"...a loving ard emotionally nuanced account of a beloved parent's descent into Alzheimer's, along with all the frustrations, sorrow, anxiety, and guilt that this terrible disease inflicted on the family. ... Readers who are dealing with a loved one's mental decline will find comfort in this sensitive and thoughtful family portrait."

Stephanie von Hirschberg
former editor and literary agent

"The treasure here is the frank portrayal of what it feels like to be the adult child of a parent who is sinking into dementia. With unusual courage, Balaban voices the anger, frustration, exhaustion, and inner conflict that bedevil many of us. But he has the gift of expressing the truth with rare insight and poignancy through his revealing vignettes, seasoned with loving tenderness and frequent doses of humor."

Anne Steigerwald
retired attorney & editor

"*Poppa Sol and Me* is a heartwarming, sometimes heart-breaking account of a man's journey to understand his father, as his father slips further and further away due to Alzheimer's. Author Richard Balaban, a clinical psychologist, shares deep, intimate insights and stories that clarify 'the value of the quality of a life and the value of the quantity of a life.' A touching example of the love of family, and the importance of compassion."

Diane David
activity director at Hospitality House nursing home

"Balaban's inner journey as he witnessed his father's decline from Alzheimer's Disease had me laughing and weeping. He brings his readers into his story with asides, sharing his innermost thoughts as the drama unfolds, a gift to us for managing our own lives. He shares parallels in his relationship with his son, and he admits to his mistakes along the way. We are immersed in a brilliant portrayal of his tragic journey. A masterpiece."

Victoria Hilkevitch Ph.D.
Professor Emerita, University of Indianapolis

"*Poppa Sol and Me* is so powerful and gripping that I ended up reading it all in one sitting. The story of Richard Balaban's journey as his son grows and his father diminishes is heart-warming and heart-wrenching and filled with honesty and love."

Steve Arnold, Clinical Psychologist

"...a beautiful and poignant story of Richard Balaban's upbringing and the ongoing development of his relationship with his father from childhood through adulthood and then through the late stages of his father's dementia. Richard masterfully weaves his childhood experience with his father's childhood experience and his own experience with his son, punctuated by the roles played by Richard's mother, wife, and daughter. I loved Richard's exploration, honesty, and coming to terms with his life viewed through this lens. I highly recommend this wonderful book!"

Amy G. Applegate
Clinical Professor of Law and Ralph F. Fuchs Faculty Fellow
Director, Civil Protection Order Clinic Indiana University
Maurer School of Law

PRAISE FOR *Poppa Sol and Me*

"...hard to put down from start to finish. Engaging and endearing, Dr. Balaban's unique writing style makes this book intimate and immediate. This book normalizes our wide-ranging emotional life, even those we label "bad." And importantly, for those dealing with their loved ones' frailties, it increases our compassion for them."

Julie Bowden,
retired psychotherapist, pioneer in Adult Children of
Alcoholics, Co-author *The Last Workshop and Recovery: A*
Guide for Adult Children of Alcoholics

"*Poppa Sol and Me* is one part diary, one part poetry, and a million parts human. It's a must read for any and all of us who might find ourselves suddenly experiencing this arduous disease journey we never wanted to be on. How beautiful to not be alone."

Darrell Ann Stone
writer, photographer, and theatre artist

"...Dr. Balaban has expressed his hope that the book might help readers in similar circumstances to find among the pathos a resembling strength, humor, and understanding. In its effort to achieve a worthy goal, the book has offered a fine and welcome work."

John McCluskey Jr.
Professor Emeritus Indiana University's African American &
African Diaspora Studies & English Department

"*Poppa Sol and Me* is not a lament for his father. The juxtaposition of the younger Poppa Sol with the older Poppa Sol was a brilliant and moving tribute, an important model for all people witnessing a loved one's Alzheimer's."

Diane Legomsky Ph.D.
retired Professor of Philosophy

"A mesmerizing, empathetic must read about a son's search for his father's soul, Poppa Sol, who is diagnosed with Alzheimer's. This poignant, thoughtful page turner about an octogenarian's predictable decline and death from dementia deeply touched me."

Ron Lustig
Attorney, retired

"Through memories and thoughtful reflection on their father-son relationship, Richard Balaban has woven an intricate and loving portrait of his father, Sol. I am deeply touched by Richard's words, sometimes sorrowful, other times humorous—but always painfully honest and true."

Dianne Haage RN, BSN

"Balaban's writing is poignant and evocative, capturing the profound changes wrought by Alzheimer's. Throughout the book, Balaban explores the disease's broader impact on relationships and family dynamics. His story is infused with moments of tenderness, humor, and resilience. ... It is a testament to the enduring strength of familial love and the human spirit."

Victor Gregor
Author *Hardened Steel: A Warrior's Odyssey*

"Balaban is an experienced clinical psychologist, and his book, told in the form of a series of vignettes and recollections, offers both compelling narrative and deep insight into the ways that families cope with the inevitable challenges of aging parents and aging selves."

Jeffrey C. Isaac, Ph.D
Rudy Professor, political science, Indiana University

POPPA SOL
and ME:
A Family's
Alzheimer's Story

Richard Balaban, PhD

Flint Hills Publishing

Cover Design by Amy Albright

stonypointgraphics.weebly.com

Flint Hills Publishing

Topeka, Kansas
Tucson, Arizona
www.flinthillspublishing.com

Printed in the U.S.A.

Paperback Book: ISBN: 978-1-953583-91-8
Electronic Book ISBN: 978-1-953583-92-5

DEDICATION

With love to my father, Sol Balaban.
The one and only Poppa Sol.

With love to my mother, Pearl Balaban.
A wise and generous woman.

Preface
Why I Wrote this Book

I began writing about my father over thirty years ago in a Writing to Heal class led by playwright, Marcia Cebulska. I needed to reduce my pain and understand my father being swallowed up by Alzheimer's—something we didn't know a lot about back then. My family and I weren't prepared for this illness that stole him from us bit by bit over the course of five years.

I was writing to save myself from the intensity of grief and anger as it became clear that I couldn't save my father. If I remained open to the fullness of my father's journey, my sadness at the loss of the man I once knew also gave rise to poignant and funny moments where his very sweetness emerged. The peaks and valleys of his decline and our father-son relationship are what I have tried to share in these pages.

Years later, I thought of this little book as a companion for those who share this life transition with someone dear to them. I envisioned one of you waking in the middle of the night, picking up this book on your nightstand, and finding comfort in reading about another family navigating similar rapids. As our family faced our limits, gained strength, and found humor and pathos, so too can your family.

September 1, 1989
Poppa Drives Right On By

It's a day like any other—an intense and meaningful one. As a clinical psychologist, I'm fully present to my clients' issues of parenting, anxiety, depression, relationships, and substance abuse. I care for them deeply with compassion and loving humor.

I don't view what I do as a job, or a profession. I'm blessed to have this "calling." I love being an intimate part of people's lives over the decades.

Twenty-five years ago, a father brought in a rebellious teenage son who had substance abuse problems and poor grades.

Today, the "rebellious son," now a responsible adult, comes into counseling with his problematic teenage son. As our session ends, I say to the father, "Let's hope your son turns out as well as you."

"Thanks. Let's hope."

As I am driving home, I find myself chuckling to myself remembering Poppa Sol declaring himself: "the only sane one in our family." Why? Because he was the only family member who had never been in therapy.

Before I know it, I'm home. I'm looking forward to dinner with Julie and our son, David.

———— • ————

3

Richard Balaban

Meanwhile, in Detroit, a small redheaded woman is standing at the window, as usual, watching for her husband to return home from work. Her relief at seeing his car making its way toward the house is quickly overshadowed by her concern as he drives past. Shortly after discovering that he has driven by, he turns around, heads back down the street, and pulls into the driveway.

She calls me in Bloomington.

"Richard, I'm worried about Poppa."

I drum my fingers on the kitchen counter.

Mom, the worrier. I can do without "Poppa trouble." I need to decompress after listening to my five psychotherapy clients.

Taking a deep breath, I ease my irritation. "You've always said, 'If you want to get something done, ask a busy man.' I'll be your busy man. Ask away."

She pauses, "You know how I stand at the window, waiting and watching for Poppa to come home from work every day?"

"I know," I say.

"You know Poppa's very thoughtful. He doesn't want to worry me. If he's running late, he exits the John C. Lodge expressway, and stops at a gas station with a telephone booth. He puts a dime in the phone and calls me."

"Was he late today?" I ask.

"No."

"So, what's the problem?"

"Today was different."

"How so?"

"I watched him drive right past our house. Straight past his very own house."

"Did he come back?"

"He did."

"So, what's your concern?"

"I think he's losing it."

"Mom, what?" *I can't believe this.* "Mom, he probably had a busy day at work and got distracted."

"I'm worried."

"Did you talk to Poppa about it?" I ask.

"No. I didn't say a word. You know, he's not much of a talker." *You think?*

"I'm sure he'll be fine," I say.

Silence.

"So, you think it's nothing?" Mom asks.

Didn't I just say that?

"Nothing, Mom. Really. Nothing."

Before

Before we knew what was happening with Poppa Sol, before we knew what we were up against, before the diagnosis and the doctors, before the devastation of dementia, before the incontinence, sexual misconduct, and outbursts of anger, before the escapes from the adult day care center and the nursing home, he was just my dad.

January 4, 1990
Poppa and Mom's Old House

The phone rings.

"Richard, isn't there a TV show called *This Old House*?" asks Mom.

"Yeah, there is."

"Let me *kvetch* about OUR old house."

Poppa Sol and Pearl in Detroit

"Complain away, Mom."

"It's driving me crazy."

"Driving you crazy?" *Okay, Richard, you can do this.*

"Everything's falling apart. If it's not a toilet, it's the water heater. Our basement flooded. No sooner did we fix that than the roof started leaking. Water, water everywhere. I'm afraid we're going to float away."

"Where's Noah and his ark when you need him?"

"You can say that again."

"That's a lot of *tsuris;* one trouble heaped upon another."

"It sure is. Four stories worth. It's hard keeping up."

"Julie and I have been trying to convince you and Poppa to move to Bloomington. You could live in a retirement community here, maintenance-free."

Silence.

"I'm not ready."

"Not ready?" I responded.

"We've lived in Detroit forever. Poppa has his office supply job. We have roots—friends, the temple. It's not so easy to pick up and leave."

"I know, Mom. It would be a big move. Just think about it."

We wanted Poppa and Mom to move to Bloomington so we could support them in their final years and so they could be grandparents to David. Amie was already a young adult.

February 1, 1990
Bloomington—Hilly? I Don't Think So

Poppa and Mom are visiting us in Bloomington. We're walking up our driveway which is slanted at about a seven-degree slope.

I ask Mom, "So, what do you think of our fair city?"

In all seriousness she says, "It's way too hilly."

Way too hilly? You gotta be kidding.

I make eye contact with Julie and decide on the spot to quit asking them to move.

February 12, 1990
Mom—A SOB?

Again, with the phone.

"Richard, our bodies, like our house, are falling apart. It's one doctor's appointment after another. If it's not our arthritis, it's Poppa's diverticulitis. If it's not his angina, it's my collapsed clavicle and lungs."

Oh my God. An organ recital.

"Poppa went with me to my doctor's appointment," Mom continues. "After the doctor checked my lung functioning, we saw him write down S.O.B. I stopped breathing for a second."

The nerve of that doctor, I thought.

"I didn't think that 'son of a bitch' is a medical diagnosis, Mom. But what do I know? I may be 'Dr. Balaban' but people let me know that I'm not a real doctor."

"Not a real doctor?" says Mom.

"I don't have an M.D. like your other son, Robert. I have a Ph.D. in clinical psychology."

"You're still 'my son, the doctor.'"

"That's sweet of you, Mom. Anyway, I'm pretty sure that *son of a bitch* is not a medical condition."

"I agree, so we asked him why he wrote S.O.B."

"What did the doctor say?"

"'S.O.B means shortness of breath. It's your major COPD symptom.' You could have knocked us over with a feather."

I laugh. "I'm relieved. With your health and the house issues, maybe it's time to move here. Think about it."

"I'll talk with Poppa."

I don't trust that they'll seriously consider it.

Their resistance to moving was based on their rootedness in Detroit. They lived there for decades. Friendships for my mother ran deep. Poppa was an usher and a member of the Men's Club of Temple Beth El where they were married and Robert and I had our Bar Mitzvahs.

Poppa Sol and Me

Post-World War II Detroit, the arsenal of democracy, had a booming economy with the highest per capita income, highest percentage of single-family ownership, and was the fastest growing big city in the country. Poopa and Uncle Nate's office supply company flourished there.

Detroit declined from 1.8 million people in 1950 to 1.0 million in 1990. Poppa and Mom didn't join in Detroit's "white flight" to the suburbs which decimated the city's overall population. The city went from the richest to one of the poorest in the U.S.

Poppa and Mom didn't talk about the changing neighborhood or moving to the suburbs. Even after their house was broken into. They never spoke of being afraid. They liked and appreciated their new neighbors who were kind and supportive of them.

Poppa and Mom and their Detroit neighbors

9

March 15, 1990
Poppa and Mom Agree to Move

We were excited when Poppa and Mom decided to move to Bloomington. Mom said that it was too difficult taking care of their four-story home. She didn't say anything about it being too difficult to take care of Poppa.

Poppa said, "We can't wait to live closer to Stephen and Michael."

"Poppa, you mean Amie and David."

"Who?"

"Stephen and Michael are Robert and Sharron's boys. You know, Robert, your other son."

"Of course, I know that."

"Anyway, Bloomington, here you come. I'm excited."

Stephen and Michael? Uh oh...

March 29, 1990
We Find Them a Home in Bloomington

Julie and I find an excellent living situation for Poppa and Mom. Meadowood Retirement Community provides a continuum of care ranging from living independently to assisted living and nursing home care. It offers educational and arts programs, a fine dining experience, medical services, and attractive grounds.

Yes!

Mission accomplished.

I can't believe we finally did it.

September 21, 1990
Poppa and Mom: The Move...Poppa's Pit

We fly to Detroit to help my parents move. Poppa gives Amie, our daughter, a tour of his basement office. Decades worth of office supply chaos lay piled up in what we affectionately call "Poppa's Pit." Overhead projectors, heavy metal adding machines, chalk-boards, mimeograph, and rolodexes lay scattered over, under, and around the ping pong table.

I walk in as Poppa enthusiastically tells Amie, "This mimeo-graph is an old-fashioned copy machine. It was called a 'mimeo.'"

"I remember that from elementary school," says Amie.

"Really. What year were you born?"

"1970."

"Photocopiers mostly replaced the mimeo around that time," Poppa says.

He goes on to describe how the overhead projector works and points out the old-style metal adding machine.

"I've saved the best for last. Amie, I'd love to show you the most interesting piece of equipment of all—this mimeograph ma-chine."

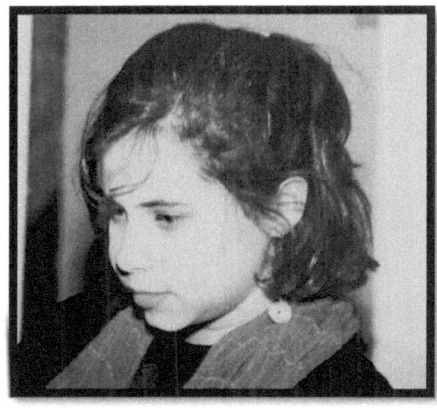

Our daughter, Amie, age 20

11

"You already have, Poppa," says Amie.

Poppa hesitates, looking a bit confused. "Just seeing if you're paying attention."

"Poppa, the jokester," I pipe in. "Thanks for showing Amie all your stuff."

"Yeah, thanks Poppa," says Amie.

October 27, 1990
Poppa and Mom: The Transition

Mom's transition to Bloomington is a difficult one. Moving from a large house to a small apartment in Meadowood, she feels closed in, selling most of her furniture leaves her sensing life is ending, not just changing. Leaving decades-long friendships is a profound loss.

Poppa says nothing about the move.

November 15, 1990
Poppa: "Give him the horn, Richard"

Years ago, I moved here from Buffalo, where beeping horns prodded the traffic forward. I was struck with how drivers in Bloomington, a laid-back university town, patiently waited for cars to go at their leisure when a red light turns green. Poppa drove in even heavier traffic in Detroit on sales calls to his customers.

Now, I am driving with him. A car is in front of us at a red light. The light turns green. The car doesn't immediately leap forward like a jackrabbit.

Poppa urges me on, "Give him the horn, Richard."

I smile to myself. *Drivers don't blast their horns here. I don't even know if mine still works.*

"Welcome to Bloomington, Poppa."

May 4, 1991
Poppa and the Racetrack

Poppa and Mom went to the Kentucky Derby today with a group from Meadowood.

I fondly remember a story that Mom told me about Poppa taking her on a date to the racetrack before their marriage. She had never been to, nor bet on, a horse race. Poppa showed her the daily tip sheet and asked her to pick winners for the Daily Double.

Mom didn't ask about the skills of the jockeys, the racing record of the horses, or how they ran on this type and length of racecourse. She read the weights—110, 118, 125 pounds—noted on the program next to the names of the horses and jockeys.

Mom was concerned that these horses must be terribly malnourished. She said to Poppa, "These horses sure don't weigh very much." Poppa smiled and informed her that the weights were those of the jockeys and not the horses.

Poppa let Mom choose her winners based on the tried-and-true method of whether she liked their names. So, off ran Ladino in the first race at 40-to-1 odds and Bloody Mary in the second at 35 to 1. Mary, is the name of Mom's sister.

Mom and Poppa cheered on Ladino and Bloody Mary to their surprising victories. Much to Poppa's shock and delight, they won over two hundred dollars.

Picking up their winnings in cash, Mom said, "My knees were knocking all the way to finding the car in the parking lot." They sped off for a celebratory steak and frog leg dinner at the Northwood Inn.

Years later, before I was born, Poppa was arrested with his Detroit bookie for illegal gambling and hauled off in a paddy wagon. As a young child hearing this story, I was fearful and fascinated by the image of Poppa, the police, the paddy wagon, and his bookie.

What kind of Poppa did I have? A notorious gambler? A wild man dancing on the wrong side of the law? I imagined enforcers showing up at our home to collect Poppa's gambling debts.

Mom gave him an ultimatum. He was not to gamble again.

And to the best of my knowledge, he didn't.

And the bookie?

What happened to him?

Serving a prison term?

No.

He became Michigan's Auditor General.

Back to the present, Poppa tells me, "The Derby was a lot of fun. I hadn't been to the races in ages, let alone bet on them."

"How'd you do?"

"Not so well."

"How come?"

"I did the betting. My mistake! I should have let Mom pick the winners."

1991

Poppa Wins the Detroit Lottery, Misses His Father

"I won a few thousand dollars in the Detroit lottery," Poppa tells me.

"Way to be, Poppa," I congratulate him.

He's now eligible to win the million-dollar Michigan lottery.

He catches me off guard by telling me, "If I win the million dollars, I would give it all up to have had a father."

I'm shocked. I've never heard him mention his father or childhood.

I'm touched by this rare window into Poppa.

Poppa looks off as if to a distant past.

1909-1917
Poppa Sol's Father and Poppa

His father was a tailor.

Sol's parents' tailor shop in Cleveland

Sol was six years old when his father died. On a gray, rainy Cleveland morning, Yiddish mingles with English in the small living room filled with mourners.

Nobody tells him but he senses his father is not coming home. Only yesterday, he saw his father putting the final touches on the Cleveland Indians jerseys.

As if from a distance, he hears people say to him, "So sorry, boychick." "He was a good man, your father." His older brothers and sisters come by and give him a pat on the head, a tickle, and a kiss.

He stands on his tiptoes looking out the window. Sol's eyes fix on the people streaming into the apartment, searching for his father in every man.

His mother is unable to financially take care of all six children.

Bottom left, my father Sol, above him is Leo, then Nate, then Phil.
Ann top right, then Sally

The three older boys go into the Jewish Orphan Asylum (JOA). The girls stayed with her.

His mother might have said, "Soly, I can't afford to feed you and your brothers."

Not wanting to be sent away like his brothers, he might have pleaded, "I won't eat much."

After living with a kind stranger for a year, he was again uprooted and told he was now old enough to join his brothers at the JOA. This was not to be a happy reunion. His mother was only allowed to visit him twice a year. This institution was underfunded through much of his stay there.

Cleveland Jewish Orphan Asylum

Five hundred children, including my father and his three broth-ers, experienced malnutrition.

Before eating lunch, he heard 500 voices chanting:

"Baruch ata Adonai Eloheinu melech ha'olam hamotzi lechem min ha'aretz. Blessed art thou Lord our God, King of the universe, who bringeth forth bread from the earth."

This prayer bounced off the walls and ceiling.

At lunch, he was faced with a watery, green-pea hash floating on his plate.

The asylum school had a more rigorous curriculum than the public schools. The JOA superintendent, a rabbi, preached about being good. His beard and booming voice were like Moses coming down Mt. Sinai bringing the Ten Commandments. Sol, listening wide-eyed, as the rabbi—without taking a breath—quickly strung together a list of values and good behaviors. Sol heard that he's supposed to help those in need, strive to improve, be honest, strong, hardworking, keep promises, control his temper, love and respect his elders, and be faithful to Judaism. Whew, almost breathless, that's a lot. He thinks the rabbi was looking straight at him. He'll try to be good.

Poppa went to bed hungry.

Hunger was his constant companion.

One of the few stories that Poppa enjoyed telling about the JOA was when he stole apples from a horse-drawn wagon. He was grateful to his older brothers who also gave him their stolen fruit.

Physical beatings were dealt out by the boys and staff alike.

Learning to be tough, he was known as "Fiery Sol."

As "inmates," they lived in dilapidated buildings overrun with rats and bed bugs. Most of the kids had lice in their hair. They bathed only once a week.

Catching and killing rats was a favorite pastime.

This photo was taken of another boy around 1916,
the year Sol entered the JOA

He left the orphanage in 1924 at the age of 15. He was confirmed on May 19, 1926, at The Temple in Cleveland by Rabbi Abba Hillel Silver who was nationally prominent in advocating for the creation of the state of Israel.

Is it any wonder that Poppa would have given a million dollars to have had a father? I would have as well.

1951

I Ask Poppa

I'm seven years old. The dining table is piled high with fried chicken, mashed potatoes, and asparagus. "I love the Detroit Lions," I say.

"They're looking good," says Poppa. "Bobby Layne is a great quarterback. Did you hear what he did when he was mad at a teammate for tackling him in a practice."

"No, what'd he do?"

"He called the next play. 'Let that guy through,' he said. The guy was let through. Layne fired the football right at his head—knocking him out."

"Tough guy," I say.

"You bet," says Poppa.

"I wanna be a Detroit Lion when I grow up."

Poppa eyes my skinny body. His fork stabs the chicken. "Good luck, son."

Questions fly out of my mouth.

"Did you ever go to a football game with your father?"

Poppa doesn't say anything.

I fire more questions.

"What was it like for you as a kid?"

"Did you have brothers or sisters?"

"What was your father like? Your mother?"

I don't wait for an answer.

He doesn't give one.

His hands start shaking. His face tightens up.

Poppa's response is harsh, terse, letting me know that his childhood is forbidden territory.

"Haven't you asked me enough questions!"

I sit stunned and silent.

I look to my mother. Her eyes focus on the food in front of her. Her head ever so slightly moves side to side. Her lips tightly shut.

Poppa stands up and hits his knee against the table.

My shoulders jump.

"I'm going downstairs to my office," he says. He leans in and gives Mom a kiss.

Mom and I finish our meal in silence.

I'm no longer hungry.

I eat anyway.

"Richard, Poppa had a rough childhood," Mom says. "He grew up in an orphanage. Best not to ask."

As a young child, how can I even begin to understand the power of Poppa's experiences in that one word: "orphanage?"

My stomach tightens. I nod. I say nothing.

I stop asking.

I don't stop wondering.

1952
Poppa Spanks Me

I fear the belt you once wielded on my bare bottom in the dank, dark basement. I cry out in terror, "Please don't hit me." Tears of shame and hurt stream molten hot down my cheeks.

"Please don't hit me again."

Mom, hearing my plea, comes swiftly down the stairs. Her face is red, matching her hair.

She scolds you, "Stop right now!"

You stop.

"Never do that again," she says.

"I won't."

You put down the belt.

You never do it again.

1961
Poppa: the Stranger

Now, I'm a teenager.

My unease with Poppa over the years and his silence about himself created a yawning chasm between us. This gap was constantly filled with a widening distance and emptiness.

I write, "Happy Birthday, Poppa" on the chalkboard in your cluttered basement office.

This man is a stranger to me.

I experience a fleeting wisp of sadness.

I stare at the words I wrote not fully knowing what a "Poppa" is.

My eyes feel heavy.

No thought occurs to me about what to do about having a father who is a mystery to me.

Twenty-two years later, my son, David, is born.

July 15, 1983
Poppa Sol is Reborn as David

"We're pregnant," says Julie. I laugh and cry. How exciting hearing David's heart beating for the first time and seeing him swim in the pool of her amniotic fluid in the ultrasound.

When I was born, fathers were not allowed into the hospital, let alone the birthing room. They stood outside. Mom yelled down to Poppa Sol the good news. "You have a son," came the word from above. "It's a boy!" you yelled to your fellow fathers. You passed out cigars.

Richard Balaban

Poppa and Mom name me after Richard the Lion Heart, King of England. He was known as a great warrior and military leader. They want me to be strong and courageous.

Richard. Richard Melvin Balaban. "Reuven Moishe" in Yiddish.

Poppa Sol holds me

When David is born, I'm right here with Julie.

No cigars.

I am awestruck, riveted, as David makes his way into this world; scrunched up from the journey. As he emerges, I'm shocked that David's wrinkled face looks exactly like my father's.

Poppa Sol is born again. *As if one Poppa Sol isn't enough for me to contend with!*

I feel overwhelmed by the responsibility of fatherhood. I'm committed to be the father to David that I wished to have had with Poppa. I wanted to have a relationship that was verbally expressive of feelings and love, and physically affectionate.

Mom was my primary parent; I'm determined to be an equal parent with Julie.

On your first night at home from the hospital, I awaken in the middle of the night. I go into your room. I don't hear you breathing.

Fearfully, I put a finger under your nose. I'm relieved to feel your breath coming out of your nostrils.

Looking at your long, thin body, I am amazed at how self-sufficient you already have become. Breathing on your own, communicating perfect y your need to be breast-fed or have your diaper changed—all by your cries. I immediately rest easier knowing how well you can be in this life.

Poppa Sol and David

August 15, 1983
Neo Nazis Set Fire to Our Congregation Beth Shalom

Exactly one month after David's birth, neo-Nazis torch our temple and burn a sacred Torah. This heinous act is recorded in the Global Terrorism Database as GTD ID 198308150012.

To this day, I am deeply touched to the point of choking up as I recall that as the fire blazed, our next-door neighbors, the president and minister of the Lutheran Church, tell us, "You have a home with us for as long as it will take you to re-build."

And we did have a home with them.

23

And we did re-build.

It is traditional in Judaism to have a baby naming. David's baby naming takes place at St. Thomas. We tell those gathered that we name you "David." David, because of its Hebrew origin meaning "beloved." David Bloom Balaban. Blessings are given for David's well-being, for living a virtuous life in accordance with Torah, for loving relationships, and for doing good deeds.

"Mazel tov, congratulations," rained down on Julie and me.

This joyful occasion arises out of the arson's ashes.

1986
David Learns a Blessing

David tells this story.

"I'm three years old.

"One night, before Shabbat, Grandma takes me aside and teaches me to say *hamotzi*—the blessing over the challah, the Sabbath bread.

"When dinner comes, I start singing the blessing before anyone else did.

"'*Baruch ata Adonai Eloheinu melech ha'olam hamotzi lechem min ha'aretz.*'

"I surprise them all!!"

Poppa, Grandma, Mom, and Dad chime in with the English translation: *"Blessed are you, Lord our God, King of the universe who brings forth bread from the earth."*

1988
I Spank David

I spank David.

I don't remember what for or why.

He's five years old.

Not only do I spank him but I'm shocked and terrified to hear Fiery Sol shoot out of my mouth. The harsh words are his; the mouth is mine. How frightening that Fiery Sol lives in me. The very Fiery Sol that I have felt afraid of.

I fear that David will be traumatized and need years of psycho-therapy.

In that moment, he charges ahead and attacks me.

Thank God he's not intimidated by me.

It looks like psychotherapy won't be necessary.

May 17, 1991
David: The Pain in the Ass

David is eight years old. He's taking his sweet time getting dressed, eating breakfast, and getting ready for school. I don't want to be late for my breakfast with Poppa and Mom at Meadowood.

In frustration, I say to him, "I've already asked you five times to get ready. Do I need to ask you ten before you get moving?"

You don't get moving. You don't answer my question.

Instead, you ask me, "Why did you have me if you knew I'd be such a big pain in the ass."

I keep myself from laughing.

"Well, how would I have known?"

July 1, 1991
Poppa, the Honest Golfer

Mom calls me. "We had a Putt-Putt tournament with other Meadowood residents."

"Sounds like fun," I say.

"It was. You'd be proud. Poppa won."

"Poppa told me that he played Putt-Putt today. He never mentioned winning." *The modest golfer.*

"They even gave him a trophy."

"That's great. He must be thrilled."

"He is, but..."

"But what?"

"He's better at golfing than adding up the score and putting the correct score in the right box."

"Did he win fair and square?"

"Of course. You know Poppa would never cheat."

"He's definitely a man of integrity."

The honest golfer.

"Something is definitely wrong with him," Mom says.

Here we go again. Give the guy a break.

"Mom, you're being overly critical of Poppa. Why make such a big deal of it?"

I hate it when Mom gets so picky about Poppa's behavior, or mine for that matter.

"I know you think that I'm being negative. I'm just being realistic."

"I know, and you think that I practice denial."

"Don't you?"

"No, Mom, I don't. I've gotten so good at denial that I don't have to practice it anymore."

I take a breath. "Congratulate Poppa on his victory."

Poppa Sol and Me

Can't add? Wrong box? Do I need to worry about our putting champion?

This conversation about golf brings back a memory from my teenage years. Poppa belonged to Tam O'Shanter, a private golf club composed of Jewish members. The name "Tam O'Shanter" evokes an image of Scottish golfers in kilts. Not so, the club was established during an era of Anti-Semitism when Jews were barred from belonging to Gentile country clubs. Poppa, member #7, and other kilt-less Jews, formed their own club.

Poppa, then in his mid-sixties, told the club champion that he was looking forward to greatly improving his game by taking lessons from the club pro. The champ replied, "At our age, the best we can hope for is to try to slow down our decline." The look on Poppa's face told me he was not fazed by the champ's assessment.

Poppa the golfer

Poppa, as a seventy-three-year-old, still played on an eighteen-hole golf course. The picture of him is competing in the Tam O'Shanter Country Club President's Day. He looked every inch the athlete in his red, black, and white plaid shirt with reddish brown pants. The golf club appears longer than he is tall. His knees are bent, his eyes are on the ball. And then, POW!

When I was a teenager, Poppa bought me a few golf lessons. I couldn't hit the ball straight. I couldn't hit the ball long. I couldn't hit the ball at all. The ball sneers at me, *Give it a try, hot shot,* knowing that I couldn't.

The game never stuck. An opportunity to play with Poppa and get to know him—lost.

July 15, 1991
David Wants to Sleep with His Mother

David was born eight years ago to this day.

I'm leading a workshop for men about being fathers at the Indiana University Alumni Family Camp.

Julie, David, and I stayed overnight for the weekend on Lake Monroe.

After swimming that afternoon, David asked me, "Why do you sleep every night with Mommy?"

I say, "When you're married and love your wife, husbands and wives sleep together."

"It's not fair," David says. "If I were you and you were me, would you like it if I slept with Mommy every night?"

"No, I wouldn't," I say.

"When you were about three years old, David, you would crawl into our bed in the middle of the night. You would cuddle up

28

with Mom with your back to me. Then, I would feel your hand push my face away."

David laughs.

"Dad, I also want to sleep with you sometimes and not just when we sleep out in our tent in the backyard."

"I'd like that," I reply.

That night, I'm reading poetry about love to David.

He says, "If it's saying, 'I love you very much,' couldn't it just say that instead of all that complicated stuff?"

July 20, 1991
Poppa's Gifts to David

Poppa Sol is giving David stamps from his own collection.

"Say thank you," I tell David.

David whispers, "He's not done yet," not wanting to stop Poppa from giving him more stamps.

July 24, 1991
Promise

David asks us, "When I grow up and have kids, will you visit me more than Poppa Sol and Grandma?"

"We will."

August 4, 1991
Poppa, Where Are You?

Poppa's sense of time and place are so distorted that he often doesn't know where he's located. We're sitting in front of Meadowood.

David asks Poppa, "Do you know where we are?"

"In Detroit," he says. "7 Mile and Livernois."

"What are we doing there?" asks David.

"Delivering office supplies," says Poppa.

Later, David asks me, "Is Poppa alright? He seems lost."

My stomach jumps. "Well, David, I grew up in the 7 Mile and Livernois area. Years ago, Poppa and his brother, Nate, had an office supply company. Poppa gets mixed up."

He sure does.

Poppa never expresses grief or loss in leaving Detroit and moving here. He never mentions missing his work, the temple, old friends, or his home in Detroit.

Why should he? He's still selling office supplies. He's never left Detroit.

"Poppa was in the office supplies business?" David asks.

So many memories come tumbling out of those two words: "office supplies."

"I'll tell you a story, David."

"Good," he says.

"It's 1933, the depth of the Great Depression. Businesses were going bankrupt right and left. Poppa and Uncle Nate started Service Office Supply (SOS) with just a $500 loan and a kitchen table.

"Not long after, SOS was also going to go bust."

"Did they?" asked David.

"The economy was in such bad shape that the U.S. government stopped paying its bills."

"Wow."

"Get this, David. Poppa wrote to President Roosevelt asking the U.S. government to pay its unpaid bills to SOS."

"He wrote the president?" asks David, looking a bit in awe.

"He did."

"What happened?"

"Believe it or not, President Roosevelt paid up."

"Poppa was gutsy," David says.

"He sure was."

"SOS went on to become the largest office supply company in Michigan and one of the biggest in the Midwest."

"Poppa never told me that," David said.

"He never would. Modesty is his middle name."

Out of nowhere, a memory arises. "As a child, David, SOS was once my playground," I say.

"What? Did it have a sandbox, jungle gym, and slide?" he asks.

"No. Not that kind of playground," I say.

I feel my joy as a three year old playing "hide-and-seek" with Poppa at SOS.

This is the story I tell David...

1947

My Playground: Service Office Supply Company (SOS)

Mom and I met Poppa at SOS before going to Joe Muer's seafood restaurant for dinner. The outer office is for retail sales of office supplies for a myriad of customer needs. In the back, the shipping department has row after row of merchandise stacked high to the ceiling.

Jumping up and down, I yell out to Poppa, "Hide and seek, hide and seek."

He is more than willing to play.

Counting aloud, "Ten, nine, eight...six, five...three two, one, zero," comes Poppa's countdown.

I run around like crazy trying to find a hiding place in this jungle of office furniture. I find a storage cabinet. Curling up in the bottom, I close the door.

Poppa's voice blasts out, "Ready or not, here I come."

My heart is beating so fast it feels like it's going to pop out of my chest. I hear Poppa yelling out, "Are you hiding behind this desk?"

Pause. "No, you're not." "How about behind this easel? Shucks, you're not."

On and on until I could barely hear his obviously-discouraged voice.

"I give up," he says. "Come out, come out wherever you are."

I don't come out.

Maybe Poppa is trying to trick me.

Poppa says, "I give up. You're too good a hider. You win."

Bursting with pride, I crawl out of my cabinet so he doesn't see my secret hiding place. Then, I run to him exclaiming, "I won, Poppa. I won."

Poppa gives me a big hug. "Yes, you did son. You did."

Mom, looks on, smiling.

"Let's go eat," Poppa says.

Hearing this story, David says, "You beat Poppa, Dad."

"I sure did."

———————— • ————————

Poppa, Mom, and I went out to dinner.

We arrived at Joe Muer's. A long line snakes from the front door. Poppa drove around back to the parking lot. We enter through the back door, walk through the kitchen, and are promptly seated.

A waiter immediately takes our order.

A red animal with claws appears on the table.

"What's that?" I ask.

"A lobster."

"It looks scary. Can I touch it?"

"Yes."

"Will it bite me?"

"No, it's dead."

I touch it. "It's hard. How can you eat it?"

Poppa shows me how to crack open the lobster. My grip isn't big enough or strong enough to crack the shell with the seafood cracker.

He cracks the shell and gives me a fork full of the soft white meat inside. It tastes delicious as it swims in a pool of butter.

Poppa happily eats the lobster. Butter dribbles down the sides of his mouth.

"Yummy," says David.

"It is," I say.

1961
Richard, The Shipping Clerk and the Long John

As a three year old, I was playing hide and seek in SOS's front office. Now, I'm a seventeen year old working in the back, in the shipping department.

I decline Poppa's offer to drive me to work. Not seeing this as a chance to get to be with him and know him, I instead take three buses and a forty-five-minute tour of Detroit each way. An opportunity to hang out with him—lost.

At SOS's shipping department, Poppa teaches me to read the bill of lading, fill the boxes, label the orders, and ship them. He artfully places the office supplies in the cardboard boxes. He customizes the boxes by cutting them down with a utility knife to precisely match the size of the merchandise to be shipped. Poppa was teaching me his blue-collar craft.

Poppa, though the boss, pitches in and is a dynamo lifting and removing office supply cartons from the opened back of railroad cars that disgorge rollers that hang like tongues.

I marvel at the strength and fluidity that flows out of his fifty-two-year-old body.

Shipping clerks take daily coffee breaks for Long Johns and doughnuts. Long Johns, usually envisioned as waffled thermal underwear, is not what we eat.

Here, an oblong custard-filled doughnut covered by chocolate frosting is a Long John.

One morning, seeing another clerk eating one with gusto, I say, "That Long John sure looks good."

"The Long John or the open mouth," he smirks.

Others laugh at the expense of this gangly, adolescent son of the boss. I cringe. I'm back being tormented by the hoods in the post-junior high boy's locker room.

Chuckling uncomfortably, I attempt to cover up my embarrassment.

The laughter screeches to an abrupt halt. Turning my head, I see Poppa, the boss, quickly walking through the shipping department.

After he leaves, a shipping clerk tells me, "Little Caesar doesn't tolerate talking during work hours."

Little Caesar, my Poppa, is also progressive. I'm proud that many years prior to civil rights legislation, he and Uncle Nate hired Donnie Crowell, a Black man, as head of Service Office Supply's warehouse to supervise all white men.

David asks, "Did you ever see Poppa in action as a salesman?"

"I did," I say. "I went on some of his sales calls. One came on the heels of Poppa potentially dying. He was a heavy cigarette smoker."

"Poppa smoked?" asked David.

"Yeah. It was at a time when cigarette companies didn't own up to the dangers of cancer."

"I thought we always knew that," David says.

"We didn't."

"Let me tell you a couple of stories."

December 3, 1971
Poppa and Cold Turkey

The First Story:

Poppa Sol with cigarette

"Poppa grew up in an era when male movie stars were pictured smoking their cigarettes. As a child, I laughed when he blew circles of smoke in my face. He smoked for decades before tobacco companies acknowledged that nicotine is carcinogenic.

"In his early 60s, he begins spitting up blood. Poppa and Mom go to Dr. Dent. The doctor says smoking is his problem: 'If you continue smoking, don't bother coming to me the next time you spit up blood. It'll be too late.'

"Poppa lit up a cigarette as he left the office. Mom didn't know if that meant he decided to continue smoking. 'I didn't say one word to him,' Mom tells me. 'I kept my mouth shut. It would only have a reverse effect if I nagged or said anything.'

"It turned out to be his last. Nicotine is as addictive as cocaine, heroin, or alcohol. The next day he quit cold turkey, against all odds. Who does that? Relatively few."

You're amazing, Poppa!

Mom diligently recorded his last smoke: 5 p.m. on December 3, 1971.

"He bought a bag of hard candies so he had something to do with his hands. From then on, he carried pocketfuls that he ate and lavished on customers."

Candy for cancer—a terrific trade.

The Second Story:

"Soon afterwards, David, I hung out with Poppa for a day as he went on his round of sales calls. I'm right behind him as he makes his entrance on the ground floor of this customer's huge business. An entire floor of forty secretaries opens up in front of us. The silence of the floor is only broken by the tap, tap, tap of typewriter keys.

"A murmur mounts into jovial noises bouncing off the walls.

"Poppa pops in.

"I hear, 'Here he comes—here comes the candy man!' The decibels grow. 'Hi, dear! Red or green?' 'You're welcome.' My pleasure,' says Poppa. Smiles, warmth, connection."

Edison invented the light bulb. Poppa expanded the limits of illumination. As he moves about, the room brightens and the temperature rises

I'm all aglow as I'm swept up in Poppa's wake.

Poppa goes on to talk with the purchasing agent. They need a paper shredder. I watch as he assesses their requirements. He discusses possible shredders to meet those needs. He tells them that S.O.S. guarantees their merchandise should anything go wrong. In addition, delivery will occur as promised. Poppa's focus is on what's in the best interest of this company and not what will bring SOS the biggest profit.

My Poppa, the salesman with integrity!

Poppa: Sterling Qualities and a Heart of Gold

Poppa was successful in business, and he and Mom were very generous as well.

In an era of antisemitism, Sol was a fundraiser for the United Jewish Appeal, a philanthropic organization that saved 162,000 Jews during the Holocaust, supported the creation and survival of Israel, and aided Jewish refugees who came to the United States.

Poppa and Mom contributed to building Mt. Sinai hospital because Jewish doctors were denied hospital admitting privileges elsewhere in Detroit. Poppa and his brother, Nate, donated desks and chairs to furnish Temple Beth El's Sunday School that Robert and I attended.

Mom tells me Poppa has, "sterling qualities and a heart of gold." She and Poppa always agreed on helping people and how much to donate. I imagine that she hopes that Poppa's positive attributes will rub off on me and my brother, Robert.

Poppa lives the JOA rabbi's message of helping those in need.

When a friend asks, Poppa and Mom came to the aid of a total stranger who was being discriminated against. Their friend, Louise Russell, teaches English to recent immigrants like Volodymyr Kovalenko, a trained electrician from Ukraine. Louise was upset when he "failed" the IBEW (International Brotherhood of Electrical Workers Union) examination for the third time by "one or two points." She felt the outcome was rigged. "His English is rough but he's a bright man."

She asked my parents for help.

Poppa and Mom learned that they can resolve Mr. Kovalenko's "problem" by making a generous contribution to the political campaign of a local judge. They do and are told, "Tell your electrician to take the exam again. He will pass, guaranteed."

And legitimately passed he did; going on to earn a living as a union electrician.

Poppa's and Mom's compassion may stem from growing up poor. Mom tells me about coming home from school and finding her family's furniture out on the sidewalk because they couldn't afford to pay the rent. Mom, like Poppa, often went to bed hungry. She was sent to Fresh Air Camp for undernourished children.

She hated choking down food to put on weight.

November 21, 1991
Poppa and the Lost and Found

I'm now at Poppa and Mom's Meadowood apartment. We are about to go to lunch.

"Poppa, what's that piece of paper sticking out of your shirt pocket?" I ask

"I don't know," he says.

"I'll take a look." Removing the paper from his pocket, I recognize Mom's handwriting.

I read aloud, "Sol Balaban, 213 Meadowood, 812-332-9200."

"That's me."

How scary. Mom is concerned that Poppa will get lost.

"It is you. If you end up in Bloomington's 'Lost and Found,' they'll return you to Mom."

"That's good."

Poppa smiles.

"Yes, it is."

"She loves me," Poppa says.

His smile broadens

"She obviously does," I reply.

"I love her too."

December 22, 1991
Poppa Takes a Nap

My parents are visiting my brother Robert and his wife Sharron and their two-year-old twins, Michael and Stephen.

I give Robert a call. "How's the visit going with Poppa and Mom?"

"It's great having them here. Strange though."

"What?" I ask.

"Yesterday, Poppa took a nap, and..."

"He's eighty-two years old. I imagine when we're that age, we'll be napping as well."

"It's not *that* he took a nap, it's *where* he took it."

"What do you mean?"

"I went to get him and found him curled up in one of the toddler's cribs. I asked him why the crib?"

How did he crawl into a crib? I wonder.

"What did he say?"

"He said it was warm."

"Wow," I responded, not quite knowing what to say.

"It was precious, endearing, and sad," said Robert. "A loving man returning to his childhood."

December 25, 1991
Christmas and Jews

It's Christmas time. I hate being invisible as a Jew during this season. David asks me, "Why do they have Christmas decorations all over town and not Chanukah ones?"

"Because there are more Christians than Jews."

"So?" he responds.

"Do you feel left out because you're Jewish?" I ask.

"No, I feel special," he says.

A bit later, David, very excited, runs to me saying, "How did they know I'm Jewish?"

"What are you talking about?"

"I was watching the Nickelodean TV show, and they said 'Happy Chanukah.'"

December 26, 1991
God and Football

David and I are watching the Indianapolis Colts football game.

"Dad, why do coaches 'thank God' when their team wins?"

I'm about to answer when he says, "And when their team loses, is it God's fault? I never heard anyone say that."

"Good point, David."

December 26, 1991
Childhood Memories with Poppa: Football

David listens as I tell him about Poppa and me playing football when I was a kid.

"We throw a football back and forth—father and son—in our front yard. The ball lands in my hands. As my arm gets stronger, our playing field extends to the Schweitzer's next door. An unwinding of my arm and legs propels the ball back to Poppa.

"He catches it one handed.

"'Great catch, Poppa!'

"He smiles.

"'Just like Doak Walker,' I say."

"Who?" asks David.

"'Who?' is what Poppa asked when he pretended not to know who Doak Walker is.

"'The Lions' halfback,' I said to Poppa.

"'Great compliment, son. I know. All Pro, Doak. That's me.'

"'Poppa;' I continue, 'The Lions will be good this year.

"'Let's hope so,' he says.

"*And they are.*

"Years later, Poppa and I went to our first Lion's game—a championship game no less!"

Richard Balaban

December 26, 1991
The Detroit Lions

I tell David that I always wanted to go to a Lions football game with Poppa. We do.

It's December 29, 1957. It's thrilling going with Poppa to the Detroit Lions championship game. Shivering in 30-degree weather, we scream at the top of our lungs, cheering on the Lions to victory over the Cleveland Browns and the great Jim Brown. It's a massacre. The Lions crush them 59 – 14.

Poppa and I congratulate ourselves.

"The Lions couldn't have done it without us," Poppa crows.

My 13-year-old magical-thinking mind agrees.

The whole drive home I'm glowing.

"We did it, Poppa! We did it!"

"Yes," he says. "We did."

We slap hands.

It's the last Lions championship. And we were there: 68 years ago.

January 7, 1992
Poppa Becomes a Multi–Millionaire

Publishers' Clearing House gives away millions of dollars to lucky winners. Who hasn't seen television ads of an unsuspecting person opening their front door and being showered with such riches?

I'm picking up Poppa at Meadowood to take him to dinner. As soon as I arrive, Poppa practically shouts, "Richard, I hit the jackpot. I won five million dollars."

"What are you talking about?"

"Here, look." His eyes light up and his face glowing as he shows me the colorful, official-looking letter.

42

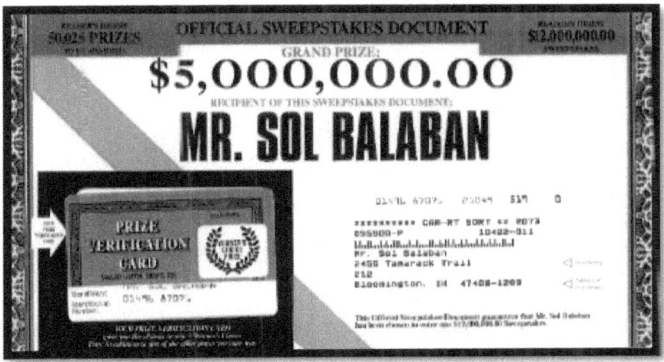

Could Poppa be one of those lucky winners?

"When I get the big bucks, Mom and I will treat you and your wife, Sharron, along with Robert and Julie and the kids to a wonderful vacation."

I decide not to correct him about who is married to whom. Matching his excitement, I say, "That would be great, Poppa."

I wade through this letter that seems to indicate that Poppa indeed won $5 million dollars. I read and read and read with nothing that hints that Poppa is not going to be millions richer.

Poppa is pacing about the apartment.

Then, much to my disappointment, I discover the truth in tiny letters I can barely read.

"Poppa, they're asking you for money to subscribe to *Reader's Digest*."

Darn.

"I won!" he insists.

I'm sure he is far from alone in believing in this good fortune.

Realizing I can't convince him, I vigorously shake his hand. "Way to be, Poppa. I'll call Julie, David, and Amie to join us for dinner."

I wait for a beat.

"Your treat!"

February 4, 1992
Two Rites of Passage; Car Keys Taken Away;
Car Keys Given

Poppa skillfully drove around Detroit for decades. But for over a year in Bloomington, he didn't know how to find his way to and from Meadowood. Mom, his co-pilot, served as Poppa's memory and map. He shows poor driving judgment. Julie, Mom, and I are in the kitchen and we agree to tell him it's no longer safe for him to be behind the wheel. I don't look forward to this conversation.

"Poppa, we'd like to talk with you," I begin. "Let's go into the living room."

"Okay," Poppa says.

"You've had wonderful decades navigating the highways and byways of Detroit as if you personally laid out the streets yourself.

Pausing, "I was always fascinated by the unique routes you carved out. I have come to do the same.

"I think of you when I'm approaching the corner of Jordan and E. 3rd street. I'm eager to get to the Indiana University Tennis Center to play doubles. If cars are already stopped at the red light on Jordan, instead of pulling up behind these cars, I make a right into the Dragon Express parking lot. I then make a left turn on E. 3rd Street, and then make a right on Jordan. This would bring a smile to my face seeing the cars that had been ahead of me were now left behind as I zoom ahead onto the Indiana University campus.

"Who does that? Poppa, you would have!"

Poppa Sol pulled similar stunts in Detroit. I enjoy this father-son connection. Does anyone else do this in Bloomington? I don't think so.

Poppa smiles.

"However, I'm sad to say you're not driving safely anymore."

Disappointment flashes across his face.

Poppa Sol and Me

"We don't want you, Mom, and others to get hurt."

"But..." Poppa begins."

"I'm sorry, but your driving days are over."

Appearing diminished, he doesn't argue.

"I don't want to give up my independence," he says. "Not being able to drive is like having an arm cut off."

His gory response hits me in the gut.

I cringe envisioning his severed arm. The arm that tossed a football around with me, bowled with me in the Detroit tournament, and slapped hands with me at the Lions' championship football game. That arm—"cut off."

Mom looks sad.

Poppa never drove again.

He taught me how to drive, tossed me the keys to the family car in my exciting rite of passage into young adulthood, and now we are taking away the keys.

Seven years later David writes his coming-of-age saga of getting his driver's license. He describes my teaching him how to drive in the parking lot of Indiana University's basketball facility. He writes, "Whenever my father would agree, we would go down to Assembly Hall where we would trade seats, and I would be in full control of the car. This was always a wonderful feeling.... I can remember stalling out about fifteen times before I was able to smoothly operate the clutch and shift gears in perfect unison."

David described drivers ed: "Whenever I went out for a drive with my instructor, he said that my skills were good, but I drove way too fast. This to me—is a great compliment. For some inexplicable reason, my parents didn't appreciate getting a call from my instructor reporting my freakish speeding habits. This, however, is all part of the ritual involved in getting a license. Parents will always want teens to drive slower and more cautiously, and teens always think they are better drivers than they really are.

"When I passed the driver's test and got my license, I had the biggest smile on my face. I walked into the DMV and told my Dad. He was excited for me.

"When we finished all of the paperwork, he handed me the keys to the car and let me drive home with him. Now that I finally had my license, I felt a great sense of freedom."

Car keys taken; car keys given.

June 25, 1992
David Wakes Poppa

We're about to have dinner. Poppa is taking a nap. "I'll wake Poppa," says David. He runs up the stairs. Shortly after, I hear a door slam. David runs down crying.

"What happened?" I ask.

"I knocked on the door. Poppa didn't answer. I went in and said, 'Poppa, Poppa, time for dinner.' He didn't say anything. I jumped on the bed."

"Then what?" I ask.

"He yelled, 'Get the hell out of here' and pushed me off the bed."

"That must have felt bad."

"It did."

"He was asleep, and you probably startled and frightened him. You shouldn't have jumped on the bed."

When Poppa came to dinner he acted as if nothing happened.

"Hey Poppa, I'm upset that you cursed at David and pushed him off the bed," I say.

"I was asleep. I dreamt I was being attacked."

"You scared me," says David.

"I'm sorry, David."

46

"It's okay, Poppa."

I'm caught between my compassion for my hurting son and my anger toward and empathy with my declining dad.

September 1, 1992
Memories from 1940: Sol and Pearl—The Honeymoon

Mom and Poppa's fifty-second anniversary is coming up. This is the story Mom told me about their honeymoon.

Pearl and Sol, early marriage

It's 1940. Sol and Pearl rode a cross-country train on their honeymoon to California. By day, they sped through the Midwest on to the Western plains and mountains. By night, the train hurtled through small towns shining like luminous pearls.

For three days and three nights they shot through time and space. Late one night, talk in their passenger car turned to the song and dance men they admired, Bill "Bojangles" Robinson and Gene Kelly.

Clickety clack, clickety clack. The swaying sound and rhythm of the train on track resonated with Sol's internal rhythm. He leapt upon a dining table and brought dance and song right into that passenger car. He did his own soft shoe while singing out of tune.

Pearl smiled shyly, blushing.

Excited and embarrassed, she looked to see others' reactions. She saw them clapping and singing.

Sol's dance flowed with the clickities and his off-kilter voice danced among the clacks. His spirit filled that car and burst out into the pitch black of night.

Pearl loved his dance and song and the electricity he created. She loved his old soft shoe and nothing else would do.

She rose to her feet and joined with others in giving him a standing ovation.

September 15, 1992
Poppa and Mom's 52nd Anniversary

The entire family is celebrating Mom and Poppa's 52nd anniversary. We go around the table and express our joy for their happy marriage. All agree that Poppa adores Mom and Mom deeply values and loves Poppa.

"Poppa," I ask, "what do you most cherish about your years with Mom?"

Poppa looks blank.

Silence.

"Poppa," David says, "you love Grandma, right?"

Silence.

Holy shit. He doesn't understand what David and I are asking him.

Mom and Julie shift uneasily in their seats.

Poppa Sol and Me

Poppa stares into space.

Mom and Poopa Sol at their 52nd wedding anniversary

October 1, 1992
I Need Healing

I need help!

I join *Writing to Heal,* a weekly class taught by the award-win-ning playwright, Marcia Cebulska.

I express my emotional pain about Poppa:

> As I experience Poppa's descent, I become more aware of my own. My hair, no longer brown or thick enough to break combs, now is grey and thinning. My limbs, no longer loose and fluid, are now achy and stiff. My body no longer carries itself with ease.
>
> The face looking back at me from the mirror more closely resembles that of my father than that

of my son. My fear is that his decline is an exaggerated version of my own. My terror is that Poppa's journey is a painful preview of my life to come.

I am closer to the end of my life than to the beginning. My youthful fantasies of greatness have gone unfulfilled. I see the arc of my life and the end of my days.

Writing gives me a creative outlet to express myself.

I USED TO BE TALL

I used to be tall, but now I'm small, shrinking into the corner of my life.

My shrinking opens my eyes to my decay. I feel less invincible.

My shrinking is aging. My muscles sag and my skeleton doesn't stand quite so erect.

My once keen memory occasionally wipes itself clean of images, names, and events.

I see my father grow smaller and smaller. His steps less sure. His words more halting and disconnected. His uncomprehending silences more frequent.

I yearn for the simple, the sparse, the bare. A sense that life is so simple as to be easily grasped with my declining capacity.

I used to fill the universe, disappearing into its every pore. Now I am melting down to my most essential self. Now I am melting down like my shrinking father.

October 18, 1992
Poppa Can No Longer Be Understood

I have been able to weave a tapestry from the multiple threads of Poppa's words to communicate with him. He is now becoming more and more difficult to understand. While each word he speaks exists in the English language, no increase of meaning comes when he puts two or three of them in a row.

Poppa's downturn eventually outpaces my ability to make whole the puzzle of his efforts to communicate.

In the Writing to Heal class, I wrote:

> *Following the gist of Poppa's words has become more difficult. I used to be able to track their serpentine, multi-layered sources, and intentions. Now, I am struck silent by his efforts to communicate. Words that follow one another don't carry meaning.*
>
> *Poppa's incoherent words and silences now stand as a pause in our family's conversation as if we collectively take a breath before carrying on.*

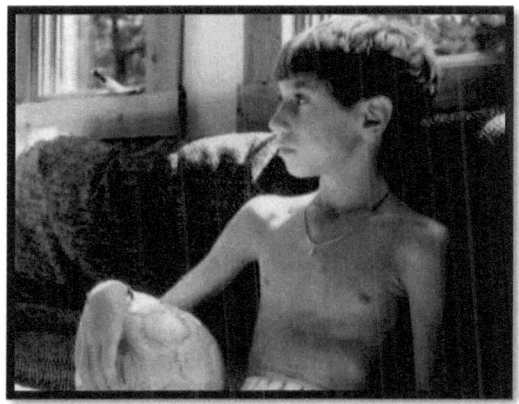

Our son, David, age 9

51

Nine-year-old David explains to us, "We think that what he says is way beyond our knowledge. He thinks we're smart enough to understand."

And we usually aren't.

October 29, 1992
Poppa is Losing It, and We Are At a Loss

At a Meadowood dinner, Mom says, "Poppa had a doctor's appointment today."

I ask, "What for?"

"It was a routine check-up," says Mom, "except..."

"Except what? I ask.

"I didn't know," she starts...

"You didn't know what?"

"That Poppa knew... "

"Knew what?" I ask. "What didn't he know?

"He told the doctor, 'I think I'm losing my marbles.'"

While aware of his deterioration, Poppa is blessed with little anxiety about it.

After dinner, Poppa and I walk back to their apartment. I ask him, "Are you worried about getting lost in the corridors?"

"No, I'm sure someone will find me."

Poppa has faith that the universe will keep him safe.

Poppa, I think to myself, *I've never heard you be pessimistic about any situation. You are an indomitable force. You have the strength to accept your circumstance and move on. Like all of us, you have your shortcomings, but you don't brood over them. You're not an introspective man. You are in the present and feel all is well there, and, for you, it is.*

Poppa Sol and Me

Our family is scared, angry, and sad because we are losing him. Would we be able to meet the needs of our Poppa falling deeper and deeper into dementia? Would we have enough patience with him? We wonder how long Mom, not well herself, will be able to care for him even with our support?

The Golden Years—Tarnished

Mom looks exhausted.

I ask her, "How are you and Poppa doing?"

Looking down at the floor, Mom says, "It's devastating. I heard of dementia. I thought he'd forget things, lose his memory. I never expected anything like *this*, not even in my wildest dreams...." Her voice trails off toward a decidedly tarnished present and future; her mouth tightens, she shakes her head.

Like this is being unable to coordinate his fingers and hands, making brushing his teeth, bathing, eating, and dressing himself nearly impossible Mom breaks down these basic tasks for Poppa. Twice daily, she tells him to pick up his toothbrush and put toothpaste on it, coaches him to brush his upper teeth, and then his lower ones.

Like this is his inability to communicate or recognize his family.

Like this is his middle-of-the-night wanderings out of the apartment, his incontinence, and occasional outbursts of anger.

It's no wonder that Mom is exhausted.

November 2, 1992
Poppa at the Hospital

After a needle biopsy, Poppa is hospitalized with a high fever.

I greet the news of possible prostate cancer with detachment. I had previously been afraid of his dying. I now more powerfully fear his survival.

I visit Poppa in the recovery room. He's still under the spell of anesthesia.

Lying in bed, he stares upward.

"What are you looking at?" I ask him.

"The Hebrew letters falling from the ceiling," he answers, as if this is a common occurrence.

"See them?"

I look up as if I too, will see Hebrew letters floating about.

He points to the door of his room. "Help! That duck is drowning in the lake."

I rush over and save the duck.

I feel like a hero.

Out of the blue, he asks if our daughter Amie's boyfriend "is being good to her?"

"He is."

Poppa's sweetness reminds me of the first time I brought Julie to Detroit to meet my parents. They greet her with hugs.

Upon arrival, Julie and I went upstairs with our luggage. That night we'll be sleeping in my old bedroom.

Later that day, Poppa, looking concerned, takes me aside.

"Is sleeping together going to ruin Julie's reputation?" he asks.

How thoughtful of Poppa.

"No more than it will ruin mine."

Today in his hospital room, I'm enjoying how verbal he is under the spell of anesthesia.

Perhaps I can slip an anesthetic into his morning coffee.

November 3, 1992
Sherbet or Ice Cream

As Poppa lies in his hospital bed, a nurse asks him, "Do you want sherbet or ice cream?"

He doesn't understand her question. He reaches out and touches the medallion on her necklace, focusing on this shiny piece of metal.

Trying to help, I complicate matters by asking her, "What kind of ice cream do you have?"

"Chocolate, vanilla, or strawberry," she says.

Poppa doesn't respond.

"Maybe you want some juice," she persists.

"What kind?" I ask.

"Apple, orange, or grape," she says.

"Apple, orange, or grape," I say to Poppa hopefully as if these same words coming out of my mouth would carry meaning for him. After many unsuccessful attempts, I give up. I say to the nurse, "Please bring him apple juice."

She does.

Poppa contentedly sips on the straw.

November 5, 1992
Angry Richard

Winter is descending. Somber gray skies and frigid temperatures yield no hope of brightness or warmth. I yearn for sunny weather and walking on a beach with Julie. Trying to plan a vacation, I find myself hemmed in by the constraints of Poppa's situation.

"I'm pissed off that we're the responsible ones, Julie," I spit out as I lean back uncomfortably on our white cotton couch.

She looks on from her cozy corner chair beneath the reading light.

She lets me know that she understands my anger.

Growing more agitated, I say, "Why did Mom and Poppa move here?"

Julie is listening.

I continue without pausing for an answer.

"Why?!"

"Because we are the stable ones. Sure, the folks could have moved to be with Robert and Sharron. But as Robert said, they may be gone in two or three years, to Seattle or Boston or God knows where.

"We're the mature adults with roots right here in Bloomington, roots that feel like concrete boots dragging us to the bottom of Lake Monroe.

"Robert and Sharron and the twins, Michael and Stephen, are coming here for four days. And who wants to give Robert and Sharron a break from their adorable three year olds? We do.

"So, can we get away for a holiday vacation? Noo-o! And as much as I love having them here and being able to do for them, **we** need a break."

The decibels increase.

"And who has been giving Mom respite from the demands of caring for Poppa? We have!"

Julie is silent.

"Just call us the friggin' *Waltons of Ruby Lane*!"

November 6, 1992
Writing to Heal Class

> *I feel enlivened as we battle Poppa's decline. I feel my rage surging. I'm boxed in by constraints that limit as well as enhance me. I love screaming out in my anger and pain.*
>
> *I love feeling an uncontrollable giddiness of being pushed beyond my limit. A powerful life force wells up in me and cascades over my brim as I laugh full bellied with tears at our human predicament.*

November 8, 1992
Relief In Sight

Poppa is released from the hospital.

My brother Robert and sister-in-law Sharron and their boys, Stephen and Michael, are visiting. We've been keeping them informed about the serious situation that we find ourselves in with Poppa and Mom. Their distance in Boston made it difficult for them to fully grasp Poppa's decline over two years. We've been talking with them about what to do about Poppa.

Robert and Sharron tell Julie and me that they would be open to Poppa and Mom moving to Boston.

"Let's talk with Mom about this and see what she has to say," I suggest.

That night, we meet with Mom.

"Mom," I begin, "we've been talking about you and Poppa with Robert and Sharron. They have some thoughts they would like to share with you."

"Okay," says Mom.

I wait, expecting Robert to take the lead.

He doesn't.

"Pearl," Sharron starts, "we'd love to have you and Poppa move to Boston. If Poppa has to go into a nursing home, you could live with us. It would be wonderful for Michael and Stephen to spend more time with their grandparents."

Robert stays silent.

Sharron continues, "Our lives would be enriched with you close by. When I go on chores or take the boys here and there, you can keep me company."

Robert adds, "Mom, it will work out well for all of us. We know you don't like being alone."

Yes!

Now that Robert has spoken, I feel relieved that our day-to-day responsibilities for Poppa and Mom will end. I'm grateful for their generosity.

"I don't want to be a burden to anyone," Mom says. "I like to be independent and do for myself."

"You won't be a burden in any way," Sharron replies. "We would be honored for you to be with us."

"I think I'd prefer staying in Bloomington at Meadowood with Sol," Mom says. "Our moving here two years ago was a big adjustment. I'm not ready for another one."

My optimism is dashed. I had hoped for a release from our burdens. I feel crushed that our responsibilities remain. A heaviness settles in my chest as I slide into exhaustion. The image of Sisyphus pushing a boulder up a hill comes to mind—only for it to always roll down again.

"Are you sure?" Robert asks.

"Yes," Mom says.

"Mom, so you're clear about what you want? You want to stay here with Poppa," I say.

Poppa Sol and Me

"Yes, I do."

Sharron leans forward, "But, you wouldn't have to live by yourself, Poppa Sol would be taken care of nearby, You wouldn't…"

"Sharron," I interrupt, "Mom knows what she wants. We need to honor her position. We don't want to be the Boy Scout intent on doing a good deed by helping an elderly woman cross the street when she doesn't want to be on the other side."

Sharron and Robert sit silently.

Julie and I make eye contact. *I wonder what she's thinking?*

She comes to me and whispers in my ear, "You look so handsome. It turns me on when you take charge."

Feeling a tingle of excitement, I turn my attention back to Mom, Robert, and Sharron.

Mom tells her oft-repeated anecdote: "A mother can take care of ten children, but ten children can't take care of one mother."

"Well, Mom," I say, "ten children can't take care of one mother when she won't let them."

A faint smile breaks across Mom's face.

She says nothing.

A frown passes over Sharron.

She too says nothing.

Robert sits back, looking relieved.

My disappointment sinks in.

Julie looks at me. We snuggle.

Our collective silence signals the end.

The end of this discussion.

The end of my hope for relief.

November 9, 1992
We're Losing Poppa

I feel sad that he's leaving me, Mom, the world.

Mom has taken more and more responsibility for his care and safety. She can't let him out of her sight. Leaving Poppa unattended even for a moment is unsafe. He might turn on the gas stove. He can't follow simple instructions like, "Sit on this bench until I come out of McDonald's." Mom once panicked when he wandered off in the mall.

I miss simple joys like watching a murder mystery with Poppa. I always marveled that he was several steps ahead of me. He often knew what would happen next and who would do what to whom.

He can no longer follow the plot.

December 4, 1992
Poppa's Dementia: My Pain

Psychotherapy and Prozac are helping my depressed clients. Prozac sounds better and better to me as my own depression swallows me up as surely as Alzheimer's is swallowing up Poppa.

My clients are getting better, but I'm not.

January 14, 1993
Writing to Heal Class

Dear Poppa:

I could kill you.

Poppa Sol and Me

I don black sweatpants, a hooded black sweatshirt, black socks, and gym shoes. Black camouflage goop smears my face.

I sneak into your apartment in the dead darkness of night. You and Mom are asleep.

Lifting a pillow, I smother you until the last gasp and shudder drain from your body.

Your soul silently hovers overhead as your final exhale hangs limp in the air.

Overcome by a sense of triumph, a pinprick of pain begins in my heart and radiates outward to all my vital organs.

Tears run down my cheeks like spring's first thaw.

January 1993

These writings help me cope by venting my anxiety, pain, and anger about Poppa, providing a temporary relief from my angst.

A more heartwarming way of adapting is to enjoy our delightful son. David's growth balances Poppa's shrinkage on the teeter totter of our lives.

David: Running with the Wind

Hair spiked and moussed.
Sinewy thin.
A ballet of movement.
Front teeth missing.
Dimples softly, happily rest upon your cheek.
Eyes full, dark brown
Open wide.
A body that moves with an awkward grace—running with the

61

wind.

One arm smoothly flowing by your side, the other at an awkward angle. Always in motion.

Flinging your body all over the soccer field. Often hurling yourself into space and finding yourself on the ground as you furiously fly after the ball.

September 24, 1992
David Plays Soccer for the Cutters

David's awkward grace leads him to play on the Cutters, a traveling soccer team. The coming-of-age movie, *Breaking Away*, was filmed in Bloomington. "Cutters" were the townies who cut rock in the limestone quarries.

David is aware of himself and his strengths and is also modest. When he was younger, he told me, "I knew I would be a good athlete when I was three. I didn't tell you or Mom because I wanted to show you and then you could see for yourself."

And he was.

And we did.

So here he is playing on the Cutters soccer team.

Even though I know precious little about this sport, I coach David's Boys' Club team during the summer. Soccer's popularity has exploded from my generation to his.

I tell David, "I'd like to sit on the bench and see how you're coached. It'll help me coach your team during the summer. Would that be okay with you?"

"No. I want you to come to watch the games from the sidelines like everyone else. You can learn by watching us play," David replies.

David stands up a bit taller.

"I can't believe I had the courage to say that."

October 22, 1992
Poppa Chases Dogs at David's Soccer Game

We invite Poppa to one of David's soccer games. I keep an eye on Poppa as he wanders about chasing and petting the dogs that families bring with them. He finds the biggest, most friendly dog, and spends the entire game talking to it, petting it, and following it around.

After a long time, Poppa asks me, "What are we doing here?"

"Watching David play soccer," I say.

"Good," he responds.

Unfortunately, the game is already over.

February 14, 1993
Enrolling Poppa in the Adult Day Care Center

Poppa's dementia continues to take a toll. We feel inadequate and guilty about needing outside support.

We enroll Poppa in the Adult Day Care Center (ADC) for people with Alzheimer's. This program provides activities for Poppa and respite for Mom and the family. Mom feels she is abandoning Poppa. I feel relieved that he will be taken care of for several hours a day, four days a week.

Richard Balaban

Collage by Poppa Sol at ADC

March 4, 1993
I Create the Character "Big Al"

Poppa Sol is dying; moment by moment; faculty by faculty. It is a dying that is insidious and painful for us. It is a dying that now spares him anxiety of his inexorable decline.

To mute my pain and develop emotional distance, I create the imaginary character "Big Al." "Al" is short for Alzheimer's. Big Al is the part of Poppa who is wracked with dementia and unable to comprehend, communicate, and function in reality.

Poppa Sol and Me

Big Al helps me distinguish the two parts of Poppa: Poppa with Alzheimer's and Poppa my father without Alzheimer's.

I give him the name Big Al even before he is formally diagnosed.

Big Al embodies humorous and quirky aspects of Poppa Sol's Alzheimer's. Big Al helps me survive the challenges of his dementia by gaining perspective and emotional insulation. I find humor, pathos, and humanity in the character of Big Al.

Big Al grows as Poppa Sol recedes.

I explain Big Al to David.

David writes about his understanding, acceptance, and love of Poppa Sol and Big Al.

Big Al and Poppa Sol

Big Al and Poppa seem to get along well.

Poppa lets Big Al see rhinoceroses in the trees; not make any sense; and just wander off in his own world.

Big Al lets Poppa Sol be intelligent, carry on a good conversation, and just make sense.

I love Big Al and Poppa Sol.

David blows me away.

Poppa was beginning to forget even places that had become familiar to him.

Last night, Poppa was at our home. Big Al says to Julie, "This looks like your place."

"It is," Julie replies.

"Where is your husband?"

Julie: "Do you know who my husband is?"

"Yes," he answers, "Lewis, who works in the office supply business."

It occurs to me that Poppa Sol's off-the-wall comments about where he is—Detroit—and what he's doing—meeting his customers or making deliveries—all involve his office supply business.

March 6, 1993
Jody and Adult Day Care

Jody, the ADC director, becomes crucial to Poppa. He comes to love her and the attention and care she showers on him.

Shortly after he joins the program, Mom finds him trying to get dressed in the middle of the night.

"Where are you going?" Mom asks.

"To Jody," he says.

Mom tells me, "He doesn't know what Adult Day Care is. All he knows is that he wants to see Jody and that's all that matters."

March 11, 1993
Richard's Support Group

I'm in a support group of mental health professionals that has met for decades. We talk about our personal and professional lives in intimate terms. I have been talking about my pain and Poppa for a long time.

In group today, I choose not to talk about my emotional pain. Instead, I focus on the positive: a pass on the YMCA basketball court from me to David for a basket; a passing from one generation to the next; my affectionate and sexual weekend with Julie.

I end by doing a graceful Tai Chi movement to express my gratitude.

March 17, 1993
Poppa Sol the Irishman

Jody tells me, "Today, your dad kept introducing himself to staff and other program participants. 'I'm Sol O'Balaban. Nice to meet you.'"

"Why did he do that?" I ask.

"It's St. Patrick's Day."

"Poppa knew better than I did."

Poppa's spontaneity of transforming himself into an O'Balaban reminds me of an embarrassing incident from my childhood.

I share this event with Jody. I'm confident she'd enjoy it.

Poppa the "Ham in Every Crowd"

"Jody, I'm nine years old.

"Our family takes the 'Maid of the Mist' boat excursion out to the Niagara River and under the falls. As our trip is ending, we're within eyesight and earshot of people in their raincoats waiting to board the ship after we disembark.

"Poppa jumps up and down, madly waving his arms. "There's a ham in every crowd and I may as well be the one," he yells.

"If I could have disappeared from the planet at that moment, I would have done so. I hid in place, hoping no one would know that he was my father."

And enjoy this story she did.

"Why doesn't your story surprise me?" she says.

"Your dad was and still is quite the character. It obviously wasn't always easy for you as his son."

"That's for sure," I say.

March 15, 1993
Poppa Makes Pudding

Jody is delighted when I tell her the middle-of-the-night story about Poppa going "to Jody." She recalls her first day with him in the program. "Shortly after we opened, Sol was the only person in attendance. I told him that I thought it would be a good idea to make dessert for lunch, and how about if we made pudding from scratch? He was good with that."

"Poppa in the kitchen?" I ask. "That was a rare sight when I was growing up. If memory serves, I only saw him boiling water once to make a hard-boiled egg."

"I guess I was in luck. He spent a long time stirring the pot. We joked and laughed and felt comfortable with each other. He can be so clever and funny."

"I'm glad he was open to developing his culinary skills with you."

"Me too!"

She hesitates.

"He would also start wondering about his ride home and if it was time to leave. But I was able to divert him. We made some tasty chocolate tapioca pudding which we enjoyed eating at lunch. I think he trusts me more because of that day."

"Chocolate tapioca pudding and popcorn were a New Year's Eve tradition in our family. But it was Mom who made the pudding."

I pause.

"You and the program have been a blessing to Poppa, Mom, and us."

"Sol is a pleasure. Thanks for sending him our way."

"Thank God you're here."

March 29, 1993
Poppa, the Kleptomaniac

When I picked up Poppa from adult day care, Jody told me, "Your Dad and Mom are really special to me."

"How so?" I ask.

"Your dad has a strong character, both humorous and determined. He can be frustrating, but he's fun to be with and a bit idiosyncratic. He likes to take things from our place, you know— magazines, pens, paper clips, stray forks or spoons, the TV remote—anything that isn't nailed down and small enough for him to put in his pocket."

Oh my.

"Poppa, the hoarder," I say to her.

"This really bothers your mom. No matter how minor and disposable the item is, she makes a point of sending it back. One day when I called, she picked up the phone, and I heard a few moments of Pearl shouting, 'And why the hell did you bring *THAT* home?'"

Then she musically spoke into the phone, as calm and gracious as ever, "Hello?"

"That's Mom for you," I say. With her social graces you would have thought she grew up a Southern Belle like Julie's mom, Fran, instead of an Orthodox Jew in the Midwest."

April 12, 1993
Poppa Takes a Hike

As I pick up Poppa from adult day care, I wonder what stories of his mischievous or problematic behaviors await me.

Today, Jody tells me quite the tale.

"Richard, as you know, this afternoon was particularly hot. Just as we finished lunch, Sol managed to slip out of the front door of our little bungalow. I saw him go, shouted to Joann that I was going to follow Sol and that the other folks in the program were in her hands, and away I went."

"Did you try to immediately get him back?

"No, I stayed at least half-a-block back so he wouldn't see me."

"Practicing your spy-craft, Jody?" I say.

"Sure was. I could see he had newspapers and magazines tucked under his arm, like a bunch of office supply catalogs. Period-ically, he would pause, look around, and continue on. He was walk-ing quite fast in the hot summer sun. I wondered if we were going to be doing this all afternoon, and I was concerned about the other participants back at the house."

I'm blown away by this story.

"Poppa sure has a lot of endurance for an eighty-four-year-old. May I be so blessed," I say.

"Well, after forty-five minutes or so, his pace was slowing and he was stopping off and on, so I decided it was time for me to mag-ically appear."

"I love your strategy."

"I acted as if I had encountered him by chance and said some-thing about what a hot day it was. He said he needed to see a cus-tomer about a sale. I suggested we go have a little coffee and pie and cool off, and then give the customer a call.

"He agreed. He was pooped! We got back to the house. He drank some water, ate some pie, and dozed in a chair until it was time to go home."

"What a story. This event could have ended badly had you not seen him leave. That's a scary thought. I'm relieved that Poppa was in your good hands."

"Thanks," she says. "After that, we put a simple hook lock on the front screen door up high enough that he couldn't reach it."

April 19, 1993
Poppa's Escape Route Blocked

I'm looking forward to picking Poppa up from ADC.

Poppa and I greet each other with a smile.

"How's Poppa doing?" I ask Jody.

Jody tells me, "Right after lunch, your dad was looking out the kitchen window. Joann was with him. She locked the back door, knowing Sol was restless. I had walked over to the hospital and was on my way back, approaching the back door, when Joann heard Sol say, 'Oh great. Here comes THAT guy. Now I'll NEVER get out of here.'"

April 30, 1993
Poppa, the Ladies' Man

Jody regales me with stories of Poppa and women. "Sol likes the ladies, especially those who are younger than he is—like the staff. He probably considers himself to be more or less the same age as us."

"Poppa has always been young at heart," I respond.

"It's not unusual for damage to the hippocampus, as occurs in some forms of dementia, to lead to a loss of impulse control and occasional hypersexuality."

"I didn't know that," I said. "Poppa was always very spontaneous, which could be either delightful or embarrassing. Fortunately, sexual misconduct was not one of his impulses."

"Sol likes to offer hugs to the staff and sneak in a little extra squeeze or two, the location of which varies depending on the lady's specific attributes," she says.

My throat tightens and my stomach jumps. To cover up my embarrassment about his inappropriateness, I say, "He's always been a touchy-feely guy."

Jody doesn't seem bothered by Poppa's behavior.

"Well, we had an open house today. Sol took it upon himself to greet the visitors. Joann's husband, Bob, walked in, smiling. Bob's a big, tall man, and Sol is not."

"Joann said, 'Sol, this is my husband, Bob.' Sol looked up at him, shook his hand, and said, 'Hi. I'm doing your wife,' and went on to greet someone else."

My dad, the ladies' man.

I'm glad I wasn't there at the time. I can only enjoy this story because the ADC staff understands the organic side of Poppa's dementia, and because Poppa hasn't been sexually inappropriate with Julie.

I decide not to tell Mom the story of "Poppa Takes a Hike" or "Poppa, the Ladies' Man."

May 3, 1993
Poppa Isn't the Only One Losing His Mind

Even with the added support of the ADC program, I continue to be emotionally depleted.

Mark Twain wrote: "Out of all the things that I have lost, I miss my mind the most." Right now, this quote applies to me as well as Poppa.

I wrote the following piece for my Writing to Heal class.

> I can't write nothing about anything. I am struck brain-dead without words coming through me to this pencil. I'm frustrated, angry, edgy; worn out, unable to give up the words or images.
>
> I hate being stuck. I haven't been able to write for a while. I may be shutting down from the agony of Poppa's decline and my mother's emotional pain and physical difficulties.

When I feel so shut down as I do now, I sometimes reflect back to Poppa's pre-dementia days. Days when we could understand what he was saying. Days when Poppa wrote so beautifully and clearly.

I remember three letters we wrote to each other. 1: Poppa, the father, encouraging me to get my doctorate. 2: Richard, the son, telling Poppa I was proud that he was my father, and I was his son. 3: Poppa, the father, saw his biggest gift to me was providing my mother as my "guardian angel."

POPPA SOL AND ME:
IN 3 LETTERS and 2 PHOTOS

1973

Letter # 1: Poppa Writes Me – "Get the lead out"

I'm slow in completing the requirements for my doctorate in clinical psychology. Poppa wrote me a letter urging that I finish my dissertation and attain my degree. Poppa was much more expressive in writing letters to me than he was in person. And I probably was as well.

Dear Son:

We, your parents, have always been proud of you and your brother. The dreams and hopes of all mothers and fathers would be answered if they can truthfully say as we can: Our sons are wonderful.

Your letter has made us both very happy.

You enclosed a copy of your Master of Arts in Psychology which fulfills step one.

A lovely secretary worked for a crusty employer. Every once in a while, he would yell at her and say, "Get the lead out of your ass." A few weeks later she came back from lunch two hours late. Her boss asked her why she was so late.

"I just had a check-up, and my doctor convinced me you were wrong and I don't have lead up my ass."

So, my loving son, I can't say you do or don't when you put off and dissipate your efforts in many directions. In many ways I'm sorry to say you are like me—not overly orderly. You get excited to start in one direction when something or other gets you going in another direction.

As I have pointed out to you, all effort must now be directed on your dissertation. No more side trips and papers for glory or publication until the above has reached a resounding conclusion.

Mother's dream of pushing you in a buggy down Dexter Avenue (the old Jewish neighborhood), and when being stopped by a friend, she would happily say: My Son the DOCTOR OF PSYCHOLOGY.

> Love,
> Dad

October, 1975
Richard Finally Gets the "Lead Out"

For as long as I can remember, Mom tells me that I'm good at listening to others, at "putting the pieces together." I am able to discover patterns in what people say, make whole a puzzle from separate incomplete pieces.

75

I'm a detective, of sorts, in solving the mysteries of feelings and relationships, which led me to become a clinical psychologist, exploring the interior lives of others.

I earn my doctorate and move to Bloomington, Indiana to head up the community mental health center's Children and Youth Service. We provide mental health services to families, like Poppa and Mom's in their childhoods, who couldn't otherwise afford them.

September 26, 1977
Letter #2: I Write Poppa—I'm Proud To Be His Son

In the spirit of my ongoing quest to get to know Poppa and emotionally connect with him, I invite him to spend a weekend with me in Bloomington by himself, without Mom. When the three of us are together, he recedes into the background.

I greet him with a hug at the airport.

"Is this a homosexual thing?" he asks.

"Nowadays, men show their affection with a hug," I assure him.

After our visit, I write you a letter.

> Dear Poppa,
>
> I loved our weekend together. You sure were vibrant and friendly at that party which was packed wall to wall with people.

Breakfast at the Tao was superb. Both Phil and Mike told me how much they enjoyed being with you and thought you were quite a guy—so do I!

I'm glad I told you that it was hurtful that you were so critical of me when growing up without a balance of positive comments. I felt great that you were so open in responding to me.

Thank you for your helpful suggestions about marketing our children's mental health services.

Playing putt-putt golf with you was a blast! You just barely beat me this time, you rascal. I'll get you next time.

I really appreciated our talk about my relationship with Sharon. You're really a no-bullshit guy.

Dad, I feel terrific that we got together. You're one hell of a guy and I'm proud to have you as my father and proud to be your son.

Love, Rich

Poppa, here it is, forty-six years later, and I discover that you had kept this letter in your desk drawer.

Richard Balaban

Poppa Sol and Me – in Two Pictures in the 1970s
A Picture is Worth a Thousand Words

May 26, 1985
Letter #3: Poppa, the Father, Chooses My Mother

Before he had Alzheimer's, Poppa wrote me a letter stating that his primary contribution as my father was to choose my mother for me.

Poppa Sol and Me

My dear son, Richard, this should have been written on Mother's Day.

I may not have been the BEST father, but I have done a few things well in my life.

1. *I chose your Mother, never forget that.*
2. *All your life from the very beginning till now, you have had a guardian angel looking after and doing things for U:*

—MOTHER—

Edgar A. Guest said it much better than I could.

Love, Dad

Here is an abbreviated version of the poem that Poppa sent me:

EDGAR A. GUEST
Father to Son

The times have proved my judgment bad.
I've followed foolish hopes in vain,....
....No brilliant wisdom I enjoy;....
But just remember this, my boy:
'Twas I who chose your mother for you!....
Your life from babyhood to now
Has known the sweetness of her care;
Her tender hand has soothed your brow;
Her love gone with you everywhere.
Through every day and every night

You've had an angel to adore you.
So, bear in mind I once was right:
'Twas I who chose your mother for you!

Poppa, you didn't give yourself credit for being a good father by your daily presence and setting a positive example for me and Robert.

I learned to translate your actions of steadfastness and responsibility into the words: "I love you." Acts, not words, were your language of love.

.

May 5, 1993
Poppa and Me: Our Differences

I continue to be totally committed to know and connect with Poppa; this man who didn't verbally reveal himself, even before dementia. It wasn't that he was deeply introspective and refused to share the fruits of his discovery. It was, as far as I could tell, that he didn't focus on, understand, or communicate his feelings.

Poppa probably was not much different than men and fathers of that era. Fathers and sons have many differences which make connection challenging. The following are some of our differences.

Poppa grew up during the Great Depression. Survival—food, shelter and clothing—were the focus. His mother and the workers at the Jewish Orphan Asylum were not inquiring into his feelings or asking his opinion.

I wasn't concerned about our family's survival needs. Poppa was an excellent provider. I could dwell inside myself and feel my sadness, pain, and happiness and reflect upon it. I intensively learned about myself in psychotherapy.

Poppa Sol and Me

It may be that Poppa's nature was more externally oriented and mine was more internally oriented.

It was hard for me to connect with this man who was so different and alien to me.

It was clear that I couldn't connect with him with words. Poppa didn't dwell there.

What is unknowable between a parent and a child?

What is knowable between a parent and a child?

Poppa was the youngest of six children.

I was the oldest of two children.

How could I ever know what it was like for Poppa to lose his father at such a tender age, live with a stranger, and then join his brothers and five hundred other children in the Jewish Orphan Asylum? The orphanage only allowed his mother to visit two times a year.

Poppa went to bed hungry. I didn't.

Poppa grew up in an environment which was physically abusive. I didn't.

How could he know what it was like for me to grow up in an intact family, in a comfortable, middle-class existence which he provided, taken care of by a loving mother and a responsible father?

Poppa Sol never flew to Paris, walked on the Champs-Élysées looking at and being looked back at by beautiful Parisian women; never took in incredible museums or came face to face with the Mona Lisa. He did not attend the theater in London. I, his son, did.

Poppa Sol never snorkeled in Sharm El Sheik before Israel returned it to the Egyptians or witnessed a bombed-out Israeli bus in the desert or cried at the Western Wall or felt that he had "come home" and knelt and kissed the ground upon landing at Israel's Ben Gurion airport. I, his son, did.

Poppa Sol never went to college, I did.

Poppa, the self-proclaimed "only sane one in the family," never experienced psychotherapy. I did; many, many years of it.

I never created with my brother one of the most successful office supply businesses in the Midwest. I didn't hire Donnie Crowell, a Black man, as the head of Service Office Supply's shipping department; Poppa Sol, my father, did.

I was not a founding member of Tam O'Shanter, a private golf club started by Jewish men who were excluded from membership in the existing country clubs that discriminated against Jews. Poppa Sol did.

And on and on and on our differences go in my continual search for understanding and emotional connection.

May 5, 1993
Son takes Deeply Demented Dad for Deep Dive of Discovery.

Poppa is rapidly going downhill with not much chance of connecting with him in a meaningful way.

Still, I can always hope.

For years I've been organizing and attending weekend men's personal growth workshops led by internationally-renowned Gestalt psychologist, Dr. Joseph Zinker. In these workshops, men open up about the most private details of their lives and gain insight and intimacy. We talk about our depression, anxiety, the challenges of our marriages, parenting, and careers.

A men's workshop is coming up shortly. The idea strikes me like a shot out of nowhere. Why not bring my father? The workshop would be an opportunity to continue to get to know him.

What a crazy idea because he's so "out of it." Dare I run it by Julie?

Poppa Sol and Me

Later that evening, Julie is in the kitchen making dinner.

With trepidation, I say, "Julie, I'm going to invite Poppa to the Zinker Men's Workshop."

Her face twists into a question mark. "Are you kidding? What in the world for?"

Poppa is rapidly being swallowed up by Big Al and it's obvious that Julie didn't consider this idea one of my best and brightest.

I couldn't disagree.

Taking a deep breath, I respond, "I can't say for sure. I know that I want him there. I know it would be like going to another planet for Poppa—just like if I attended one of his office supply conventions. I still need intimacy with him, and I want to give it a shot during the men's weekend."

As her eyes fix upon me, I feel I am "sprawling on a pin...wriggling on the wall," as described by T.S. Eliot.

"Julie, I just want him there with me."

"Richard, we can barely understand him. What is it going to be like for him and the other men?"

I don't say anything.

Later that evening, I tell Poppa, "Remember the times I invited you to visit me for a weekend in Bloomington? Just you and me without Mom, 'A men's weekend?'" Without waiting for a response, I move closer and hold Poppa's hand.

I continue, "I'm so glad you came. I always had a wonderful time with you."

A smile spreads across his face like peanut butter smeared across Wonder Bread.

"I want you to come to a men's workshop with me. I would love you to be there with me and the other men."

"If you want me to, I will," he says.

May 15 – 17, 1993
The Men's Weekend: Poppa's Blessing

The men are very caring—walking Poppa from one session to another, supporting his unsure steps.

I glance over and see Poppa slide into a nap during an afternoon session. As he sleeps with one arm in the air, Eric, another participant, holds Poppa's hand throughout the doze. Eric and Poppa are backlit by the sun enfolding them in a warm yellow glow.

At that moment, it came to me. What does a child want most from a father? What does this son need from his father?

The answer: His blessing.

As another man finishes talking about his relationship with his father, I barrel ahead without guidance from Dr. Zinker.

Before asking for Poppa's blessing, I share a couple of precious experiences I had with him as I was growing up.

"Poppa, I have an early memory of playfully wrestling with you as a four-year-old. Mom was concerned for my safety but we 'men' ignored her and had our fun.

I tell him this story...

1948
Poppa and I Wrestle

"You and I were wrestling with each other on our living room floor.

"I hurled my body with all my might against your strong, muscled one. I used all my strength. You met my power with equal power and no more. I never gained an advantage, and you never took one. I loved matching my strength against yours.

My hands pushed against you. I loved my body squirming about your body.

"We couldn't stop laughing.

"You were not only playful but fiercely protective of a friend of mine who was being hurt by his father as they wrestled.

"Years later, I watched my friend, Alex, wrestling with his father.

"The father, Ron, viciously twisted Alex's arm. Alex yelled out in pain.

"The father demanded, 'Give up.' Alex refused.

"My friend turned away from his father and held back his tears, his face red with anger.

"I'm shocked. Sick to my stomach.

"You, Poppa, jumped in between them. Your face right in Ron's. You didn't say a word. The veins on your neck looked like they were going to burst. It looked like you were going to explode Fiery Sol all over Ron.

"You growled, 'Stop, Ron. You're hurting the boy.'

"Ron saw the look on your face and your body ready to pounce.

"He stopped.

"Poppa, you were my hero!"

I see a faint recognition crossing Poppa's face.

Looking around the room, the men are riveted by this childhood memory.

I go on to tell Poppa one more story. Another father-son story that is dear to my heart.

Richard Balaban

1949
I'm Five Years Old — You Teach Me

"You took me to Palmer Park in Detroit to teach me how to ride my two-wheeler Schwinn. Running behind me, you held me and the bike upright. The sun was beating down and the wind was blowing in my face. I pedaled as fast as I could. My legs tightened. I'm flying! Turning around, I was surprised to see you far behind me. You'd let me go.

"You said, 'Let's keep this a secret from Mom. We'll show her next week that you can ride all by yourself.'

"I nodded. A smile stretched across my face.

"Next week Mom came with us to the park.

"I was thrilled to show off my brand-new bike riding skills.

Mom was beaming.

You were proud."

When I finish telling these stories, Poppa smiles.

"Poppa, I'm so grateful that you're my father. It wasn't always easy. Sometimes I was afraid and even embarrassed by you. But you're a good man with a good heart. You did your best and I couldn't have asked for more. Hopefully, David will say the same about me."

I pause.

"I hope you feel that I was a good son."

Poppa nods slightly.

Now, I move next to him.

Poppa Sol and Me

I say, "I need your blessing for me as a loving husband, father, and psychologist."

Gently helping him to his feet, I raise Poppa's arms in the position of a rabbinic blessing over my bowed head and bent knees.

I pause before going on. Something is missing. I think about how Poppa is an uninhibited and lively guy, a Jewish Zorba the Greek. I want to be more like him in this way.

So, I add, "I also want your blessing to help me become more spontaneous and energetic—just like you."

Poppa says nothing. He tilts his head and looks at me. I read approval in his eyes. With an open heart, I receive his silent blessing. In that moment I feel a loving completion of my relationship with him.

I move closer.

We hug.

I hear the men applaud.

I feel full looking around the room, surrounded by smiling, caring male energy.

At the weekend's close, the men express their appreciation for what they experienced. Some are disinterested in getting together with the other group members in the future.

Mike says, "I had a great weekend, but I really don't have much time for contact after the workshop." Joe, nodding his head, agrees, "This is one of the few times during a year that I allow for emotional intimacy with men and that's okay." Larry shakes his head in rebuttal. "I'm concerned with how quickly we're de-constructing the weekend."

Silence.

Discomfort and tension ripples through the group.

More silence.

Poppa speaks up with a solution in a surprisingly complete sentence. "Well, if you're walking down the street and see another man from the group walking toward you, you can just cross over to the other side."

Peals of laughter shower on Poppa, for the wisdom of our tribal elder.

His words draw the workshop to a close.

Postscript to the Blessing

"Poppa's Blessing" completed an emotional connection with him that I so desired for decades. From that moment on, I felt a deep gratitude, with no regrets, about our relationship.

Years later, I asked Julie, "How was it that I was freed at that moment?

Julie helps me see the obvious that eluded me.

"You were the one who gave yourself the fatherly blessing," she said, "and it was you who received the blessing!"

I agreed with her. Now, I fully understood. Poppa was more than a willing participant, and for that I am deeply indebted.

May 22, 1993
Poppa Sol and Big Al, Confused and Loving

Sometimes Big Al confuses two events that happen in proximity.

Poppa and Mom watch Oprah's show about husbands who abandon their wives. Hours later, when I arrive home from work, he sees me hug and kiss Julie.

Big Al, with tears in his eyes, says to Mom, "He came back. They still love each other."

June 29, 1993
The "TV Man" Steals the Remote Control

Big Al begins inconveniently hiding things.

One night, Mom says to Poppa, "I can't find the remote control for the TV. Do you know where it is?"

Big Al denies losing it and explains, "I saw a man step out of the TV set and take it."

Unfortunately, Big Al can't remember where the "TV man" put it.

August 2, 1993
Big Al and Finances

In a family discussion about a recent financial scandal in the news, Big Al, looking at Julie's green sweater, says, "It was the Irish who did it."

"Yes," I say, "they made off with all the greenbacks," *as if they vacuumed out all our savings accounts.*

Julie's eyes meet mine in acknowledgement of my desperate attempt to incorporate Big Al's comment into our conversation.

October 6, 1993
The Diagnosis

We have Poppa evaluated at the Alzheimer's Clinic of the Indiana University Medical Center. The diagnosis: *Moderate senile dementia of the Alzheimer's type, bordering on the severe.*

While no surprise, there it is, the diagnosis.

That night, at dinner, Poppa's hands are in constant, chaotic motion. It is upsetting to watch him fidget non-stop, folding and unfolding a napkin over and over again, and aimlessly moving his fork and knife around the dinner table.

Julie suggests harnessing his energy by wrapping a package as he did so adroitly in shipping office supplies. I think back to working as a shipping clerk at Poppa's company when I was seventeen. Poppa taught me how to expertly pack and ship merchandise.

To put Poppa's hands to work, I set up a box and got items like a stapler, tape, several pads of paper, an appointment book, pens and pencils.

It breaks our hearts to watch Poppa awkwardly crease and crumble paper, trying unsuccessfully to fit objects into the box. Thirty minutes later, after great persistence, he walks off as if he wasn't even engaged in this task.

October 7, 1993
Cognex Gives Us Hope

Shortly after the diagnosis, we made an appointment with a neurologist, Dr. Somers. He prescribes Cognex, the recently-approved and sole Alzheimer's medication. We're hopeful that this drug will slow Poppa's decline. For a brief while, we think we notice an improvement.

Mom later tells me that she didn't tell Dr. Somers about Poppa's masturbation.

She hadn't told me either. I didn't know.

Mom wondered if we should tell Dr. Somers. "Maybe he can give Poppa medication for it."

"I wouldn't want to take away Poppa's pleasure," I say.

"I know. I just want to be honest," she says.

November 14, 1993
Subconscious Speaks

Robert tells me Poppa said, "Sometimes they neglect me. I'm not a lost soul."

November 15, 1993
I Dream of Golf Balls

Poppa has been hallucinating golf balls for several months now.

I dream that Poppa is dragging around clear plastic garbage bags.

"What are you doing, Poppa?"

"Nothing."

"What's with the garbage bags?"

"It's for golf balls."

"What golf balls?"

"The ones around."

"Around?" I say. I find myself looking although I know there are no golf balls to be seen. Maybe I will see golf balls when I awaken from this dream.

"Let's go into the kitchen, Poppa." I take him by the hand and lead him there. I see shattered glass on the reddish-brown quarry tile floor. A broken pitcher lies like a sunken ocean liner run aground by the crimson garbage can.

"What happened?" I say aloud not expecting an answer nor waiting for one. I stare silently at the glass sparkling like tiny diamonds. Turning away, I look at my father who is no longer behind me.

Poppa is lying down on the broken glass—his body gray, pale, naked. Poppa picks up a piece of glass and begins cutting himself on his inner thigh. No blood emerges, no mark appears.

"Stop!" I yell as I lurch to grab his arm with the broken piece of glass in it. He's now sitting behind me on a ledge looking down at me.

"Poppa," I say, bewildered.

He looks at me full in the face saying, "If I had a gun I would put it in the right place."

A shiver runs down my back as I see the dead serious look on Poppa's face.

November 15, 1993
Poppa and Julie

Julie went to wake Poppa from a nap. She helped him to a seated position. Before she could react, he kissed her with an open mouth, and kissed her on the neck. When he stood up, he pressed his pelvis against her.

Startled, Julie pulled back. She noticed that he had an erection. For just a second, she felt like shoving him away. But instead, she thought how confused he was, and how embarrassed he would be when confronted with what he did.

When I come home from work, Julie tells me about what happened with Poppa.

Julie and I had learned about the organic links between hypersexuality and dementia. Julie experienced Poppa's sexual behavior as that of Big Al while I responded like it was the behavior of Poppa Sol.

She was not upset. I was.

I'm angry. My protective instincts kick in.

Poppa Sol and Me

I confront Poppa, "Do you remember kissing Julie this morning?"

"We're lovers," he replies.

"Don't you dare kiss Julie like that any more. You're still married to my mother. You're not lovers," I emphasize, "Your wife is your lover and Julie is mine. Mom's your wife and Julie is my wife, so *hands off*!"

In that moment I realized that I was the one who lacked empathy and understanding. Julie had been violated and here I was "protecting" her when she had already handled the situation to her own satisfaction. She understood that this man sometimes couldn't even tell you his own name or what state he was living in, and here I was verbally assaulting him.

Verbally assaulting my own father.

That night at dinner at Meadowood, Poppa approaches Julie with his arms wide open. I grab him roughly and stand between him and Julie in the buffet line. I'm not going to have a repeat of his earlier transgression.

Later that night, I said to her, "I feel bad about the way I manhandled Poppa."

"I felt protected," she said.

"From moment to moment, we don't know what we're going to encounter with Poppa. It's confusing and upsetting." I paused. "Next time, I'll just try to be firm and not so aggressive."

My wife, Julie

Richard Balaban

November 22, 1993
Poppa and the Platter

We're having lunch at Meadowood.

Poppa is sitting next to our daughter, Amie, age 23. He's cutting up her meat. Amie is a college student. She learned to use a knife long ago.

In the middle of our conversation, he gets up and walks over to the buffet line. We watch as he picks up a huge platter of tomatoes, onions, and lettuce and brings it over to Goldie Newman.

As I rush over to rescue the platter, I hear him say to her, "Here's your lunch, Goldie."

"Thank you, Sol," says Goldie. "But that's way too much salad for me."

I say to Poppa, "That's very generous of you to bring all that salad over to her. That platter is bigger than she is. Let's take it back to the buffet table and rejoin the family."

Poppa takes my hand and comes along with me.

1960
Poppa and a Platter from the Past: A Memory

Another platter comes to mind from my teenage years.

Poppa spins in his own orbit, saying and doing whatever strikes him in that moment.

Decades ago, I'm a teenager witnessing another episode of Poppa being uniquely himself.

Our family is having dinner at Tam O'Shanter. Poppa is the last to go through the buffet line. I look up and see him twist his wrist beneath the plate, overflowing with food, in a downward gravity-defying spiral. Bringing it to a stable upright position, he then glides his food, totally intact, in for a miraculously safe landing on our table.

I gasp.

People at an adjoining table applaud.

Do I give him a standing ovation or duck underneath the table?

November 28, 1993
Bowling

Poppa, David, and I go bowling. Poppa surprisingly retains some of the good form that he displayed years ago in the bowling alley. So much so that, while Poppa is deep into his dementia, David tells me, "He looks more like a normal person bowling; not like someone with Alzheimer's."

"Funny you should say that, David," I begin. "Let me tell you a story about Poppa and me and bowling."

"Tell away, Dad," says David.

March 1963
Poppa and I Knock 'Em Down

Poppa and I entered the Detroit Father and Son Bowling tournament.

I showed David a picture of Poppa, the lefty bowler.

I say, "Note the balletic form. Perfect symmetry of left arm and left leg parallel to each other at a graceful 60-degree angle, balancing his delivery of the ball. Head still, focusing on the target, a strike in the making."

"He looks like a pro," says David.

"That form and determination helped propel us to proudly finish in second place of hundreds of entrants in our division in the Detroit Father and Son Bowling tournament.

"Our pictures were in the *Detroit News.* I bowled the best set of my life—210, 172, and 187 for a total of 569. Poppa did almost as well at 562."

While we enjoy knocking over a whopping 1131 pins, the real fun is being exuberant teammates—Poppa and I cheer each other on, handshakes, smiles, laughter, pats on the back and "atta-boys" as we flood the lanes with strikes and spares. I can still feel the excitement and warmth over six decades later—one of the most vividly fun moments in our relationship.

"Wow, Dad," David says, "that's probably better than we could ever do."

And it is.

Poppa the bowler

November 30, 1993
Luck

Out of the blue, Poppa tells me, "I have all these people taking care of me and I don't have to pay them anything."

"You're one lucky guy!" I say.

December 2, 1993
I Love...I Hate

In my Writing to Heal class, Marcia gives us a writing prompt: "What I love and hate about our family, winter, and the holiday season."

I love David being so insightful, compassionate, and loving with Poppa.

I hate the rain that batters our roof, causing leaks in the solarium, dining room, and living room.

I love when Poppa's love shines through.

I hate that Mom is suffering from Poppa's decline.

I love my parents' love for each other.

I hate the cold in my bones and the stiffness in my joints—the fear that I will be taken before my time—frozen in place—unable to thaw.

I love venturing out into the cold night to see the brilliant stars in the clear sky and the lunar eclipse slicing the moon piece by piece.

I hate the black ice that sends me flying, landing on my butt, banging my head on the ground.

I love the beauty of sparkling ice on trees and the snow gently blanketing the ground.

I hate feeling hopeless and exhausted.

97

I love Julie and her powerful presence in being
so supportive of me and being so loving of Poppa
and Mom.

1993
Prediction

David is ten years old.

I overhear him and his cousin Matt talking.

David: "Masturbation is the next best thing to sex."

Matt: "How do you know?"

David: "I'm just guessing."

December 9, 1993
Diminishing Dad, Expanding Son – Loss on Both Ends

I'm having brunch at the Uptown Cafe with my dear friend, Bob
Weiskopf.

"What's up?" asks Bob as we sit down in a booth.

"David just flew for the first time by himself. Picking him up at
the gate, he sprinted out of the plane and leapt into my arms. A
flight attendant says to me, 'I guess I don't need to check your iden-
tification.'"

I laugh, experiencing the loving warmth of my blur of a leaping,
hugging son.

I explain to Bob, "Julie and I are eager to hear about David's
solo flight and time with his cousins Matt and Jackson in Chicago.
As soon as we get home, David wants his best friend, Zach, to spend
the night with him. David senses that I'm upset.

"He asks me, 'What's wrong, Dad?'

"I tell him, 'I'm only a little sad. I wanted our family to be together on your first night back.'

"'I'm very sensitive,' David says about himself. 'I wish I wasn't so sensitive, because it keeps me from doing what I want to do, like seeing Zach. Sometimes, I have to do what I want to do and forget all that sensitive junk. It's not that I want to exclude you, Dad. You can play basketball with me and Zach at the Y if you want.'"

I add another packet of turbinado sugar and half and half to my coffee.

Bob smiles, "Did you say yes to David?"

"I told him, 'Call Zach. We'll play ball. He can stay over.'"

"He said, 'Thanks, Dad,' David's eyes were sparkling.

"I felt a tug at my heart. I'm so proud of him for being so aware of his needs and feelings and speaking up for himself. I'm also feeling less essential and central in his life even as I'm so proud of him for growing up and away so wonderfully."

"What deliciously conflicted feelings," says Bob. "I feel the same with my Emma and Daniel. Kids grow up so quickly. First, you're changing their diapers, then they are crawling around on the floor, and then, before you know it, you're driving them off to college."

I look out the window at the traffic going by.

"So true."

I take a breath.

"I'm caught between my diminishing father and my expanding son. I'm losing my father day by day. I'm losing my centrality to my son. Death inhabits both relationships—one is excruciatingly painful, and the other is a mixture of pride, joy, and loss. Some of it wondrous and aching and some sad and heart breaking."

"That's confusingly complex," says Bob. "What else?"

"It has to do with mini-grieving, loss, and letting go. It has to do with accepting, appreciating, and celebrating what is and grieving what is not as well."

I take a breath. "It has to do with becoming more. Poppa and Mom's situation requires that of me. I'm saying goodbye to my more stingy, fearful, and self-centered self, and hello to the more giving and generous *Mensch*. A dying and birth within myself."

I see Bob listening carefully.

I stop and pour more turbinado cane sugar into my coffee. This "sugar in the raw" brown packet joins a sizable stack on my side of the table.

"So, you're talking about transformations, transitions, beginnings, and endings," Bob says.

"Yes." I nod.

Bob nods.

With that, Bob and I sit in silence, drinking our coffees.

December 30, 1993
Nursing Home: The Decision

Even with the support of adult day care and public health nursing, taking care of Poppa is a much greater challenge than Mom and our family can meet. Cognex has not held back the ravages of this disease.

Mom comes over to the house, sits down on the couch and tells Julie and me that she is no longer able to care for Poppa in the apartment. She tears up. "It's too much. I think it's time for him to be in a nursing home," she whispers.

"You have done the best you can," I say, "for as long as you can. You're overwhelmed and need a break."

Julie reaches to hold Mom's hand. I feel a knot in my stomach.

Poppa Sol and Me

"Richard," Mom says, "I know that you've been saying it would be a relief for me to not have to take care of Poppa, and I ought to consider having him go into Bloomington Convalescent Center. You've been concerned with my health—the high blood pressure, feeling faint, the pain from my fall and broken ribs. I just needed to do all I could, by myself. And I think I have. Now, I think it's time."

"Mom," I say, "this must be hard for you to acknowledge."

"It is."

"Mom, you're incredibly responsible and on top of things."

Her eyes moisten.

"If it weren't for you, Poppa would've been in a nursing home ages ago. He's totally incapable of taking care of himself. You've always been a giver, Mom. Always looking out for the needs of others and never focusing on your own," I say.

Mom shifts about on the couch.

I continue, "It's extremely difficult living with Poppa. He never was much of a conversationalist, but now when he speaks, he often can't be understood. He also tests your patience when he can't do seemingly simple tasks. He challenges your sense of control when he does things that bother you and behaves inappropriately."

"It's been hard."

"I don't know how you've managed. You've done the best you can. When do you want to get things moving?"

"As soon as possible," she says.

"Ok, I'll call Bloomington Convalescent Center."

We had done research about nursing homes and chose BCC as the best fit for Poppa. It's operated under the auspices of Bloomington Hospital. We had spoken to them months ago, but Mom was not ready at that time.

I get up from the couch and call Marilyn, the BCC admissions person. "My dad continues going downhill and Mom is overwhelmed. He goes to adult day care three or four days a week and public health nursing bathes him three times a week. Even so, it's too much for her."

"We don't have an opening on the intermediate care floor," she reports, "but you could begin the admissions process. You need to call Area 10 Agency on Aging to certify that your father requires nursing home care. Also, his doctor needs to fill out the admission forms."

"Will do."

I find it helpful having clarity about the next steps I need to take.

While trusting we've made the right decision, I also feel sad.

That night, David senses that I'm upset. "What's wrong, Dad?"

"I'm sad that Poppa's going into a nursing home."

"Me, too," David says. "I won't see him as much."

We cry and hug each other.

Over the next week, I take care of the necessary requirements. Now we wait.

Deciding to put Poppa in a nursing home is a heart-wrenching, complex process. We did the best we could but caring for Poppa is too great a challenge for our family.

Julie and I are concerned that Poppa will suffer a significant setback in the nursing home. He is already disoriented enough. He regressed when he moved to Bloomington and then again when he was hospitalized. I'm afraid he'll feel abandoned like he was as a young child.

Alzheimer's is already a formidable, if not insurmountable opponent. Adding a possible regression may well reduce the possible effectiveness of Cognex.

Is the improvement we think we notice the medication or our wishful thinking? After several weeks, I ask Mom how Cognex is working. Mom says, "Poppa's more talkative with little coherence, more facially expressive, and more defiant, which I don't need."

"Sorry to hear, Mom."

"Mensch tracht un gott lacht," she says.

"Yes, I know," I say. "Yiddish for 'Man plans and God laughs.'"

Still, we try to be optimistic and remind ourselves that Cognex may require eight to ten more weeks to work. We want to give Poppa the best possible chance that the medicine will restore some functioning.

Julie and I decide to provide more support to my parents until BCC has a room for Poppa. Being supportive of them has been incredibly demanding but hasn't totally disrupted our lives. This will have to change.

Before dinner, we ask Mom to talk with us.

I begin, "Mom, you have done an incredible job taking care of Poppa. Julie and I don't know how you did it."

Mom is listening closely, not saying a word.

"Julie and I want to give you much more support. We will have you and Poppa over more during the day and overnight several times a week I will sometimes spend the night with Poppa at Meadowood while you get a break and a good night's sleep at our home."

I can see Mom's shoulders drop a bit.

"We're open to whatever other ideas you have. What do you think, Mom?'

"I think it's a good idea, Richard. Let's give it a try."

"Good. I'll tell Marilyn from BCC of our plan."

"Are you sure?" asks Mom.

"Definitely," I answer.

That night Poppa will sleep in our daughter Amie's old room as she is away at college.

I ask David, "Would you be open to Grandma sleeping in your bed tonight so she can be across the hall from Poppa Sol? We won't ask you to do this every time, but we would appreciate your help."

"Where do I sleep?"
"You can sleep in our room in your sleeping bag."
"Okay."

January 9, 1994
Poppa and Me: Snapshots

I'm not always a loving son.

Today, Poppa, again, took a variety of objects from ADC. I'm angry and grab them roughly from him. I say in a harsh voice, "Don't take things that don't belong to you."

"All right," he says, "don't be so mean."

Later that night, I'm driving Poppa to Meadowood to spend the night with him while Mom takes an overnight break at our home.

At the entrance to the parking lot I ask, "Can you find your way back to your apartment?"

I know he can't.

I want to humiliate him.

"Do you think I have some screws loose?" he asks.

Yeah, I think to myself.

"Get out and walk down the walkway. I'll meet you after I park the car."

I look on as Poppa can't locate the car door handle. He reaches for the cigarette lighter. He pushes the button to the glove compartment. He extends his hand vaguely into space.

I let him fumble around for a while. My stomach aches. I grip the steering wheel.

"We'll park the car and walk in together," I say.

"Thanks, son."

"Here, let me open the door for you, Poppa," attempting to redeem myself.

Poppa's hands come to a rest on his lap.

Up in the apartment, Poppa is aimlessly pacing. I say, "Poppa, sit on the toilet so you can go before hitting the sack."

I bend down and remove his shoes, socks, and diaper.

After he urinates, I put a new diaper on him that I taped together.

"First the right leg, Poppa."

He lifts his right leg.

"Good," I say as he puts his leg in.

"And now the left one."

He does.

"That's great."

"Now let's pull the diaper over your cute little *tushie*."

Poppa does a little jig to wiggle the diaper in place.

I feel a sense of joy and satisfaction as I play back scenes of David's infant days when I undressed, diapered, and dressed him.

Changing David's diaper was a surprising pleasure as he stared up at me. I sang, "Bup Meister General, Bup Meister General" as he smiled and cooed. Nothing could be better.

I, the father, diapered my son, David. And now I, the son, am a father to my father, Poppa Sol.

January 11, 1994
The Car-Driving Dog

I'm driving Poppa to Meadowood to spend the night with him. Mom is staying at our house. Out of the corner of my eye, I see him smiling. "What are you smiling about?

"Didn't you see that dog driving that car that we just passed?"

"No, I must have missed it."

January 14, 1994
I'm Drained Emotionally and Financially

Supporting Mom and Poppa is frustrating and consuming of time, emotion, and spirit. I'm feeling drained. It's one thing piled on top of another—going to Poppa and Mom's doctor's appointments, meetings with adult day care staff, and deciding on a nursing home.

I'm financially jeopardizing my family.

I don't have the energy and time for my private practice.

My earnings have fallen to their lowest level in a decade—a level I can't afford to continue; a level at which I can't support my family.

January 1994
Death by Freezing

The *Herald Times* reports that an old woman in Bloomington died in freezing weather while walking her dog.

I fantasize driving Poppa far out into the countryside, leaving him to wander to his death. I've heard that freezing to death is a painless, peaceful way to go—drifting into a dreamlike state and coma.

February 11, 1994
Poppa and Love

"Poppa, what is love?" I ask.

"Love is hearing bells," Poppa says, "You have to make sure the right person hears the bells with you."

I tell David Poppa's definition of love.

"Oh my God," David says. "That's good; probably better than whatever you might have said."

"You're right," I say. "Poppa amazes me sometimes."

"Me, too."

February 13, 1994
Poppa's Wisdom and Sensitivity

Interspersed in the difficult times are moments of clarity; enjoyable moments that we cherish.

Julie to Mom: "Do you want to go shopping with me at Target?"

Mom: "No. I probably shouldn't. My back is hurting."

Poppa: "It will probably hurt more if you stay here."

February 14, 1994
Richard: Loyal Son

Poppa: "Are you coming home tonight?"

Richard: "No," I say, tongue in cheek. "I think I'll go out to the bars tonight. Maybe pick up a woman. Is that okay with you?"

Poppa: "That's not good."

Richard: "Would you like me to stay at home?"

Poppa: "Yes."

Richard: "Okay."

Poppa: "Good. My loyal son."

February 15, 1994
Poppa is "With It"

Julie and I are taking Poppa and Mom back to Meadowood after they spent the night with us.

I'm feeling impatient as Poppa takes a long time to get into the car because he doesn't know how to maneuver his body into the back seat.

Finally seated, Poppa talks aloud to himself. "Ho, ho, oh, Balaban. They think you've lost your marbles. But they don't know that you are more with it than most of them in this car."

February 17, 1994
Poppa: Union Man

Richard: "Poppa, your nephew's boss fired him after working on the job for two years just because he left work early one day."

Poppa: "Didn't he belong to the union?"

I imagine that Poppa's question stems from his Detroit days during the heyday of the automobile unions: the AFL-CIO and the UAW.

I'm taken by surprise when Poppa seems to make sense, responding like his pre-Alzheimer's self.

Am I reading too much into his few words, wanting desperately for him to be lucid?

I remember back many years when Poppa was the one who was fired.

1962
Poppa is Fired

After selling your office supply business, you work as a salesman for another company.

I'm eighteen years old.

One night at dinner, you tell Mom and me, "I got fired today."

You express no shame nor humiliation about the firing cr security officers walking you out of the building. I listen as you and Mom discuss getting a job from the contacts you built up over the decades. I'm impressed that you and Mom approach this issue as a problem to be solved rather than an exercise in self-pity, bitterness, or blame.

You must have felt confident we wouldn't think less of you. As for me, just the opposite.

I've read about men who were so ashamed about being fired that they pretended for months to go to work to a non-existent job.

Poppa, you are always positive in the face of adversity. You work hard and love your work. You come home for our sit-down family dinners. You're an exemplar of having a good work-family balance— much for this teenage son to strive for and admire.

Back to the present...

February 26, 1994
Poppa's Ready for the Nursing Home.

For three demanding months we provide added support to Poppa and Mom. We want to keep Poppa out of the nursing home by giving Cognex time to work. Caring for Poppa and supporting Mom is more than our family can adequately manage.

Marilyn, BCC admissions person, calls us about an opening. This time Mom is ready. My brother Robert and his wife Sharron come to Bloomington to help with Poppa's transition into BCC.

I bring Poppa and Mom to our home to see Robert and Sharron. They hadn't seen Poppa for several months. What they observe helps ease our consciences.

Poppa is significantly disoriented with respect to people and places. When we get in the house, Poppa looks around and insists, "This isn't your house. Your house is down the street."

Several times he walks outside, attempting to find "our house." I take him by the hand and point out all the things he should recognize both inside and outside our house. He would have none of it.

Poppa's agitation grows. "I don't want to stay here because this is not your house. I'll show you in the phone book that Balaban doesn't live here."

David, trying to calm him down, says, "I live here."

"Get out of here," Poppa yells, "or I'll kick you in the ass."

David is alarmed and cries.

My whole body tightens.

Mom, who never heard such hostile talk from Poppa in fifty-three years of marriage, bursts into tears.

Robert, Julie, and I, three veteran mental health professionals, are jarred by Poppa's unbridled emotion.

"I guess Poppa's ready for the nursing home," wryly concludes Robert, the psychiatrist.

Any remaining feelings of guilt about our reasons for putting Poppa into a nursing home are alleviated.

That night after Poppa and Mom left, I felt angry, devastated, hopeless.

February 27, 1994
Mashed Potatoes – My Fantasy

I write "Mashed Potatoes" as a Writing to Heal class exercise.

Mashed Potatoes

We're having a family dinner with Poppa and Mom. Looking across the dining table, I see Poppa's blank look of total absence. After saying a blessing, I fire a handful of mashed potatoes at Poppa's face. I still have a strong throwing arm. It lands full on. He barely twitches, his eyes blink.

"These sure are delicious mashed potatoes," I say to Julie. "Thanks, hon."

"You're welcome. Glad you like them," she replies.

Mom is upset with me. "That wasn't nice, Richard. Look what you did to Poppa. What did he ever do to you to deserve that?"

"You're right," I say. "I don't know what got into me."

"Poppa," I ask, "how was adult day care today?"

"The people seemed to be floating about," comes his garbled response. "The dog ate all the golf balls."

"Sounds like a fun day," says Julie, patting Poppa's hand.

"David, please eat your peas and potatoes," Julie says.

"I will, Mom," he sighs. David slides his peas under the fish and spreads the mashed potatoes around his plate. He longs for the days when Sadie, their cairn terrier, hung out at the dinner table and rid his plate of damning evidence. Those days are gone.

I take another huge helping of mashed potatoes and playfully squish it through my teeth.

David is looking hopelessly at the peas and potatoes on his plate.

Mom looks with concern at Poppa's mashed potatoes-face.

Julie looks with disapproval at me.

Poppa moves the mashed potatoes about his face trying unsuccessfully to locate his mouth.

Another typical family dinner, I think to myself, as we all quietly finish our meal.

Whatever became of my living our family's rule, "If you don't have anything nice to say or do, don't say or do it?"

February 28, 1994
Poppa Visits the Nursing Home

The pre-admission visits to the nursing home are filled with anxiety and sadness. Could we have done better? Will they take good care of him? Will he vegetate? Give up and die?

And the relief. Will we be able to think and feel about matters other than Poppa and Mom? Can we stop worrying all the time? Can we begin enjoying ourselves again?

We bring Poppa to BCC and introduce him to the Intermediate Care Unit staff.

That night, when tucking Poppa into bed at Meadowood, I say, "This new place will be good for you."

"I think so," he responds, "They seem nice and act nice. t's a place for people who make mistakes with their pills."

We made our decision.

Now we've got to make it work.

I'm hopeful.

March 3, 1994
Difficult Decision

"Mom, you're looking better," I say. "That's because you and Julie are taking such good care of me." My stomach tightens up, not wanting to ful y let myself feel this warmth. I'm fearful that she will need too much. In her loneliness, fear and poor health, Mom may want to move in with us.

I'm not ready for and don't want that. I feel guilty about feeling this way. Poppa and Mom took in my Grandma Rose, Mom's mother. I am not going to take Mom in to live with us.

In this way, Poppa was a better son-in-law than I am a son.

I feel particularly bad because I loved Grandma Rose and have fond memories of her which go back over four decades.

1950
My Roommate, Grandma Rose

Richard Balaban

Grandma Rose comes to live with us. After my brother Robert is born, she and I share a bedroom.

One day, I'm surprised to see an absence of hair under her armpits. Too shy to ask her about it, I say, "Grandma, let's exercise."

She smiles.

"Follow me," I say. "Put your right arm up and bring it down. Now put your left arm in the air and bring it down."

Grandma mirrors my motion. I sneak a look at those smooth, bare underarms and marvel at this miracle of nature.

Yiddish was Grandma Rose's first language. Her English, while passable, was a work in progress.

I always got a kick out of this story.

Mom is Grandma's translator when she writes letters to relatives. Grandma dictates a letter in Yiddish. Mom transcribes it into English. Grandma wants to end a letter with a blessing for her relatives. She says, "May God blast you all."

Mom transcribes it as dictated and sends the letter on its way.

One day, I come home from school, mad. I feel like yelling at my friend. Grandma speaks to me in Yiddish "Oh, shayna yingele..." and more." I ask her what she's saying. She translates: "Sweet young boy. Watch what you say."

"What do you mean?" I ask.

"When the words are out of your mouth, the other person is boss over them."

I don't want anyone to be boss over MY words.

I'm being encouraged into silence—in Yiddish, no less.

Grandma Rose died when I was eleven years old. I told Mom, "This is the saddest day of my life."

Even such warm and loving memories do not lead to my wanting Mom to live with us.

And so it is that Poppa goes into the nursing home and Mom continues to live at Meadowood.

March 7, 1994
Poppa Enters the Nursing Home

Mom tells Marilyn, "Poppa masturbates every other day." Mom wants to be honest but is concerned that they will not take him.

Much to Mom's relief, Marilyn says, "The staff is used to it. Some patients do it daily."

Hoping for the best, we check Poppa into the Bloomington Convalescent Center.

A patient, hunched over, walks past us.

In a very small voice, Poppa says, "Decrepit."

Julie, not quite hearing, asks, "What?"

"It wasn't nice what I said. But she's decrepit," he replies.

Poppa says to a nurse, "Be nice to me, because I pay the bills."

The nurse asks, "What do you like to do?"

Poppa: "I like a woman, but I'm private—the same woman."

Robert: "Mustang Poppa!"

Poppa tells the nurse about Mom: "She knows every move I make. She puts it into her little book."

When Robert and I leave, Poppa says, "It's a sad moment, my sons leaving me."

Poppa looks at me. "Will you visit me?"

"A lot," I reply.

Poppa: "I didn't know that you loved me so much."

As Mom and I leave BCC, I say, "Mom, I'll get the car and pick you up at the front door."

As I walk to the car, out of earshot of Mom, I find myself screaming at the top of my lungs, "YES!" I ball up my fist and throw it up in the air. I'm excited that we are taking this huge step after many intense and exhausting months.

I'm surprised that Mom doesn't want to stay for dinner with Poppa and immediately agreed to a DNR—Do Not Resuscitate directive—to let Poppa slip away if he is not able to survive on his own.

I think of T. S. Eliot's lines:

This is the way the world ends.
This is the way the world ends
Not with a bang but a whimper

Driving Mom to Meadowood, she says with a wavering voice, "Don't get so close to that car, Richard." A pause. "It's not you, it's me. I'm nervous."

"Are you relieved not to have to take care of Poppa?" I ask Mom. "Dress and undress him; get him into a diaper; give him his meds?"

"Yes and no," she says. "Yes, when he is not cooperating and is giving me a hard time. On the other hand, I will be lonely by myself."

Later that night...

Julie asks, "How was it leaving Poppa at the nursing home?"

"Much better than our fears," I begin. "I don't remember if I told you what Doug, our son-in-law, said when we visited him in Palo Alto?"

"What did he say?" asks Julie.

He said, "Poppa is softer and more emotionally expressive than when you were growing up. He became tough to survive his traumatic childhood. Now, he's vulnerable, more emotionally open and expressive of his love."

"This is something I wanted when I was younger," I say. "I remember a lobster dinner when I was three years old. My hands weren't strong enough to crack the lobster's outer shell to get to the sweet meat inside. But now Poppa's hard shell is softening, and his sweetness is emerging."

"Interesting metaphor, Richard," replies Julie.

"It's been percolating in my mind for a while, I hope it's not too contrived."

"No, sounds good," Julie says, "And I know how much you love lobster. We don't get much of it in land-locked Bloomington."

"No, sadly we don't," I say. "We had to go to Maine to get our fill."

March 10, 1994
Mom's Tears

Mom stays with us overnight. She sleeps until 10:00—an extremely rare and obviously well-needed rest.

Mom tells me, 'I want to visit Poppa."

"You must be feeling much better. Are you?" I ask.

"An hour and an hour."

"If you're not much better, you shouldn't visit."

"There is the physical part and there is the emotional part and I want to see him," she tears up, almost crying.

"Have you cried during this time?" I ask.

"No."

"Do you feel sad?"

"It's stuck in my throat."

March 10, 1994
Poppa in the Nursing Home

Mom and I are visiting Poppa. A nurse tells Mom to only visit Poppa one or two times a week to give him a chance to adjust here and to give her a break to take care of herself.

As I say goodbye to Poppa in the nursing home, I kiss him on the forehead. "I love you," I say.

Poppa smiles.

I smell a waft of urine as I leave.

"Ooh, ooh, ooh," comes a trilling patient's voice.

This disembodied sound surrounds me. A chill runs up my spine.

"Ooh, ooh, ooh," echoes down the hall from the day room—the day room where the white-haired women hang out.

"Ooh, ooh, ooh," follows me as I make my way to the elevator.

A white-haired woman in a wheelchair reaches out to grab at me.

I pull away to a safe distance. My stomach jumps.

"Ooh, ooh, ooh."

I descend to the first floor.

"Ooh, ooh, ooh."

I find my way home.

March 12, 1994
Holding Hands with Poppa

I try my best to adapt to being with Poppa at BCC. I hold tight to at least one experience from each visit that is touching or humorous.

I feel Poppa's soft, warm hand. Holding his hand, I slow up my pace. I hold his hand to lead him to places he cannot go by himself—to his room, to sit and talk, to tuck him in for a nap or bedtime.

He is lost in space. He is lost in time. He is lost in the here and now.

March 13, 1994
Adjusting

Mom and I are visiting Poppa. We see he doesn't know how to do basic things like pulling the cord to get help or finding his way to the bathroom.

We share this concern with his nurse who says, "Most of our patients are like him. We're very adept at handling things. It will take two weeks of mistakes to set up his routine."

I'm listening carefully to what she is saying.

The nurse taking care of Poppa continues, "This staff has a reputation for treating their people well. I've already had people say about your father, 'Thank you. Thank you for giving us a good one.' I'll write out your feedback and attach it to his chart. It may help smooth out some of your worries and help inform our staff. We'll introduce your father to other male residents."

I shake her hand and thank her for listening and telling me about how they operate.

Mom and I go to talk to Poppa who tells us, "There are a lot of women here who are disturbed, and you can't understand them."

"That must be hard for you," Mom says.

"I've got a lot of clothes here and you might want to take some home because I don't know how long I'm going to be here."

Mom and I are struck that Poppa strung together so many words that are coherent.

Mom tells me, "The Cognex must be working."

Sad.

He's NOT coming home to Mom.

March 14, 1994
The Invisible Lady

I'm trying my best to take whatever pleasure I can from being with Poppa.

Poppa's roommate, Jeff, comes into their room with a grin and hello for Poppa.

"The smiling man," Poppa says cheerfully.

"Is your wife here today?" I ask.

"Can't seem to find her," Jeff replies as if his wife were his frequently-misplaced pair of glasses.

"She'll find you," I say.

"The invisible lady," chimes in Poppa.

March 16, 1994
Love and Fevers

"I love you, Poppa," I say.

"Thank you. You make me feel like a man again." Poppa continues, "One of these days I want to come to you. Or you can come to me and I will... We are living in the strange business of fevers and medications, and I don't like it."

March 19, 1994
Loving Poppa

At dinner, Poppa's roommate spills his coffee.

"It's okay," says Poppa as he gets up to help him clean it up.

When it's time to leave, I kiss Poppa on the forehead.

"I love you," I say.

"I'll take all the love you give me."

March 20, 1994
Poppa Gives a Blessing

Julie tells me about her lunch with Poppa and his roommate Jeff, a retired preacher.

Everyone waits for Jeff to say grace. He bows his head. He stammers and stutters. He struggles to say a prayer he cannot remember.

Silence surrounds his tears.

Poppa says, "As long as you have breath in you—and body and soul—you'll make it."

With Poppa's invocation, everybody begins eating.

Julie sits and weeps, unable to eat.

March 21, 1994
Poppa on the Lam

After a visit with Poppa, Mom says to Julie and me, "I have a strange feeling that Poppa's going to leave BCC today."

"What are you talking about?" Julie asks.

"Mark my words," she prophesies, "he's going to get on that elevator and walk out."

That evening I'm with Mom in her apartment.

The telephone rings.

I pick up and a voice asks, "Does Sol Balabee live here?"

"He did. Why?" I answer.

"I'm officer Woods, Bloomington Police Department. I have him over here at Pizza Hut."

"Oh my God. What happened?"

"We got a call that Mr. Balaboo tried to buy a pizza with a Sports Illustrated subscription form."

"Is he alright?"

"Chipper as can be."

"Phew. That's a relief. I'll come get him."

"Good. Mr. Baladoo. Your father is really out of it."

I hang up.

"Who's that, Richard?" Mom asks.

"Bloomington police."

Mom, her face drains of blood, hand shaking over her heart, says, "That's just what I need to hear. Police—and Poppa out of the nursing home.

"Mom, he's fine. You were right. He took a trip to Pizza Hut. I'll get him and bring him home."

I leave Meadowood feeling strong, singing along with Nylon's music: *That's the sound of the men working on the chain gang.* Thank God he's safe. I would have felt quite differently had we received a call from BCC that Poppa is missing.

I pull up behind the squad car.

"Richard," comes Poppa's cheerful voice.

"Hi, Poppa." Giving him a kiss on the cheek, I feel the roughness of the stubble on his face. "Quite an adventure you've had."

He smiles.

"Thanks for rescuing Poppa, officer," I say, shaking his hand.

"All in a day's work," he replies.

"Let's go back to your place," I say to Poppa.

I reach out to him.

He holds my hand and follows along.

March 22, 1994
The Electric Razor Telephone

Seeing that Poppa needs a shave, I hand him his electric razor.

He puts it to his ear and mouth.

Hello," he says, "Hello. Anyone there?"

Oh my, Poppa thinks his razor is a phone.

I'm taken back to a childhood memory of standing in front of a mirror in the bathroom while Poppa shaved with shaving cream and a razor while I had a toy plastic razor pretending to shave.

I felt so grown up.

March 27, 1994
Problematic Poppa

Although he didn't complain to us about being at BCC, it was clear that he was unhappy there. Mom tells me, "I got a call from the nurse at BCC. She said that Poppa had been aggressive for the last forty-five minutes. He tried to hit some of the aides. He is walking around with his coat and hat and is trying to get out."

We are terrified that BCC will kick him out of their facility. And then what will we do?

April 7, 1994
Triumph

I write this piece for my Writing to Heal class in response to our terror of Poppa possibly being kicked out of BCC.

Triumph
On a high cliff I stand as a lone figure etched
dark against the sun rising.

A day of struggle. I am not accustomed to being denied. "No" means nothing to me except the next challenge to push and persevere to "Yes."

I am determined to find a way through, around or over.

The sun sets. In the blackness of the night, I imagine myself being tossed about in the ocean below—feeling a sadness with no images—a pure sensation of watery pain.

I know I will awaken with energy renewed for the battle. I will carve out a path no matter what.

The sun rises.

April 10, 1994
Poppa is Substituting

We could usually cherish one small interaction in our visits.

I am visiting Poppa at bedtime.

"Put on your PJs," I say. "They're on your bed."

"Those aren't mine," he replies.

"You sleep in that bed, Poppa."

"No, I'm substituting for the guy who sleeps there," he insists.

April 17, 1994
Poppa Loves Mom

Mom has been sick.

I took Poppa out of BCC for a short visit. I tell him, "Let's pick up Mom. The doctor says she's doing better."

"I feel a tingle in my heart and breast to hear she's doing better. I want to give her a kiss and a hug."

We drive to pick up Mom. As Mom gets in the back seat, Poppa asks me, "Can I sit in the back with her?"

"Of course," I say, walking around the front of the car to help Poppa settle in next to Mom.

"Can I give you a hug?" Poppa asks her.

"That would be nice when we get to Meadowood," she replies.

I pull the car in front of Meadowood.

As they get out, Poppa stretches his arms wide and shuffles toward her.

They kiss and hug.

"I love you," whispers Poppa.

"I love you too," says Mom.

Mom and Poppa Sol love each other

That night, he tells me, "Even if we only speak nonsense, I still like talking with her."

Richard Balaban

April 20, 1994
Poppa: "I'm getting ready for the days ahead."

Tonight, Julie tells me about a conversation she had with Poppa in the nursing home earlier in the day.

Poppa: "I'm getting ready for the days ahead."

Julie: "What days?"

Poppa: "When I won't be here any more."

Julie: "Are you ready for that?"

Poppa: "Yes, I think so. I'll miss Robert and David and the twins."

Julie: "Are you feeling tired?"

Poppa: "I don't have energy any more. I love Pearl most of all."

Julie: "It's good that you can say how you're feeling."

Poppa: "Yes."

Julie: "Are you sad?"

Poppa: "A little."

When she's finished telling me the story, Julie touches my hand.

While I am moved by this story, my jaw tightens, and I explode. "Really, Julie? He'll miss Robert most of all? What about his other son?"

"His other son? What other son?" laughs Julie.

"Poppa and Mom only had two sons."

"Oh, my husband?"

"The one whose life is being swallowed up by Poppa's dementia," I say.

Julie and I burst into laughter.

"Tough luck, soldier," she says. "No good deed goes unpunished."

April 25, 1994
Poppa: BCC Board Member

The lines between fantasy and reality are often blurred with Poppa. We learn to flow with it, and sometimes we even enjoy the ride.

Poppa and I are having lunch. He tells me, "I've been made a member of the BCC board. They took out the old timers and elected me. I was there for a few hours yesterday."

"That's great, Poppa. Congratulations."

"The staff wants a fifty-cent per hour raise and I said I'd look into it and see what the going rate is."

We are heartened by Poppas' warmth and compassion. His story seems so real. For a split second I feel proud of Poppa for being made a board member and imagine him gathering information to benefit the staff.

I quickly realize that this story is a complete fabrication. A caring fabrication, at that. How does he make up this stuff whole cloth?

May 1, 1994
Poppa Compliments a Nurse

Poppa says to nurse Linda: "You have nice lines down your side backs."

Linda: "Thank you."

Poppa: "You're welcome."

May 4, 1994
Poppa, the Mathematician

After dinner with Poppa and Julie's parents, Julie says, "I'll take Pearl and my parents home. Richard, you take Poppa to BCC."

Poppa: "I'm equal to three people."

Despite these isolated delightful moments, we continue to receive calls from the nursing staff that Poppa is restless and combative. He craps on himself, craps on the floor, strikes out at staff, or crawls into other patients' beds. We are appalled because this is not the Poppa we knew and loved.

We fear that his behavior will jeopardize his stay at BCC.

When visiting him late in the morning, we find him lying in bed in his pajamas. Staff report he doesn't want to get up. He's uncooperative. Personal items like his clothing, his shoes, glasses, or false teeth are often misplaced or lost. His pants are ill-fitting from the weight he has lost. More and more he takes on the appearance of a hopeless, warehoused patient.

Being with Poppa is like "one mini death piled atop another; one period of mourning followed by another."

It tears at our hearts to see his halting, shaky walk, to hear him continue to speak a language we can't understand, to feel his little body, weak and unsure, and to know that if we inhaled deeply enough, we would be smelling death.

August 1, 1994
Poppa Breaks his Hip

Mom, the eternal secretary, writes down messages from her answering machine. She entitles them: BLOOMINGTON CONVALESCENT CENTER: RE: SOL BALABAN

I get a kick of her labeling her notes with Poppa's full name as if she didn't know to whom these notes refer.

"Monday, August 1, I received a message on my answering machine: "It is 12:30. This is Pauline from BCC calling. Sol fell and he was taken by ambulance to the emergency room. Dr. Jim Rickert, an orthopedic surgeon, looked at the X-rays and said he fractured his left hip and needs surgery."

We're on vacation. Learning about Poppa, we cut our trip short and head back to Bloomington.

We find him in the hospital, agitated and disoriented, not recognizing any of us.

August 2, 1994
Poppa has Surgery

Mom's notes: "On Tuesday, August 2nd at 8:30 p.m., Dr. Rickert did a left hip replacement, & admitted him into the hospital."

"Sol was discharged on Wednesday, August 10th and went back to BCC."

August 16, 1994
Poppa Back to Emergency Room

Mom's notes: "I received a call from BCC saying the physical therapist noticed there was something wrong with the hip and sent him by ambulance to the emergency room. They took X-rays and Dr. Rickert said that the hip is out of the socket. At 7:30 p.m., Dr. Rickert put the hip back into the socket. He was admitted into the hospital."

August 20, 1994
Poppa Discharged

"On Saturday, August 20th at 2:00 P.M. Sol was discharged and taken by ambulance back to BCC."

August 22, 1994
Poppa Back to the ER

Within two days of being discharged, he dislocates his hip again.

Mom's recording: "I received a call from Cora (Charge Nurse) at BCC saying it seemed as though something was wrong with the hip and they sent him by ambulance back to the emergency room at about 12:00 noon. They took X-rays again and Dr. Rickert said that the hip is out of the socket again and sent him to the surgery department. 7:00 p.m. Dr. Rickert put the hip back into the socket in the surgery room."

When his hip dislocates for the third time, it becomes clear that enough is enough. We talk to his surgeon, Dr. Rickert, about how to immobilize Poppa's hip. We all sense that he may not be able to heal. The body needs a cooperative partner who can remind the body what healing requires. Poppa is no longer able to be that partner.

Mom's summarizing notes: "Was back to BCC from August 10th to August 16th—hip goes out.

From August 20th to August 22nd—only 48 hours at BCC and the hip goes out again."

August 24, 1994
My Thought

I think to myself: *The only good news left is for Poppa to die.*

August 25, 1994
Poppa and the Value of a Life

Our journey with Poppa helped us clarify the value of life and the value of death; the value of the quality of a life and the value of the quantity of a l fe.

Julie helps me understand that life is not necessarily good, and death is not necessarily bad.

I begin to realize that our goal is not to extend the quantity of Poppa's life when the quality of his life runs out.

It is a complex issue because Poppa is in no position to judge the quality of his life. Further, Mom has been paying a heavy emotional and physical price for Poppa's "life."

In this context, death is a deliverance. Death is a relief, a release, a blessing. Death, when it comes to take Poppa, will give us back our "life."

August 28, 1994
Poppa Nears the End

It's becoming increasingly difficult for Poppa to be able to eat. Sucking through a straw is a complicated procedure for him.

Julie, Mom, and I visit Poppa at the hospital. A loud gurgling noise emerges from his lungs and mouth. We hear the dreaded death rattle.

A nurse's aide proudly tells us that she fed him a whole meal after he had barely eaten for days. We're appalled. He's not capable of chewing, and the food went to his lungs. Doesn't this well-meaning "angel of death" realize that this may well shorten Poppa's life? He is drowning on his evening meal.

The nurses try aspirating the fluid in his lungs, but he develops a fever and lapses into a coma. His breathing is labored.

"His temperature is not yet a pneumonia fever but close," Dr. Rickert says. "I'm going to call another physician who will prescribe antibiotics and steroids."

"What will happen if he's not treated?" I ask.

"He will most likely die. Even if treated, there is no guarantee he will survive," he says.

I remember my conversation with Julie about the quality versus the quantity of a life. I snap back into this moment, and to the doctor's words: "Even if treated, there is no guarantee he will survive."

My stomach jumps.

"Let's go into another room and talk," I say, knowing that we will begin a conversation that will determine the fate of my father. Even though he's in a coma, I don't want to have this discussion in Poppa's presence.

"Mom," I say, compelled by an inner voice. "I don't want us to treat this infection with antibiotics or steroids. If Poppa's body can fight it off, that's fine. I know my father. He's a vital, passionate, in-the-moment man, and there is nothing left for him here. Not in this life. Not anymore. He wouldn't choose to live this way. My hope is that he goes peacefully and painlessly, that he suffers no longer, and that he moves on to wherever he is going."

I look outside.

Thick, darkening gray clouds are swirling, moving swiftly, churning.

"Mom, this is your decision, but I wanted to let you know how I feel. What do you think? Do you want Poppa to be treated?"

Calm, Buddha-like, Mom's answer is firm, gentle. "No way. I just don't want him to suffer."

Dr. Rickert is comforting as well as realistic. "If you make the decision not to proceed with medication, there is no turning back. I would give him intravenous hydration, pain medication, and oxygen, which will help him breathe easier."

"How long will he last?" I ask.

"He could go as soon as a day, perhaps longer."

We went back to Poppa's room. His breathing is labored. I tell him, "You don't have to stay here for me. You can go if you want. I love you."

"Mom, say goodbye to him," I say. "Tell him all the ways you love him."

Mom says goodnight to him. I'm touched as I watch her stroke his arm and the hair on his head as she talks lovingly to him.

Later that night, I return to Bloomington Hospital to sleep in Poppa's room. The nurses have moved him to a private room, knowing that we will need the space to be with him as a man letting go of his life. And, we letting go of him.

"I knew you would be back," says the nurse.

"Why?"

"Because if that was my father, I would have done the same thing."

The nurse is most caring and accommodating to me. She shows me how the chair converts into a mini bed, gives me apple juice, covers, and a pillow.

Poppa's ragged, labored breathing sounds like angels singing, calling to Poppa.

This is Poppa's last night. I just sense it.

August 29, 1994
Poppa's Last Morning

When I wake up in the morning, I tell the nurse that my brother and his family would want to be with Poppa if it looks like the end.

"You should give him a call."

I do. Robert says they will fly in tonight.

As I begin to leave, the nurse says, "The doctor ordered us to turn off your father's oxygen."

"Now?"

"Yes."

"Would it be alright if I do it?"

She nods.

"Will you show me how?"

She does.

I take a breath.

My hand shakes.

I twist the dial.

He's been in a coma for over a day.

Before leaving the hospital, I hold Poppa's hand, not wanting to let go. I whisper, "Poppa, I love you." I recall for him a special memory. "Remember teaching me to ride a two-wheeler bike? You held on to the seat of my Schwinn at Palmer Park. I pedaled as fast as I could as you ran behind me. I didn't realize it, but you let go of the seat. I pedaled on alone.

"You asked me not to tell Mom. 'It's our secret,' you said. I kept it. The next weekend, I loved seeing the look of surprise on her face as I rode my bike all on my own. Thanks for teaching me and then letting me go, Poppa. I love you."

As I left, I stroked his hand. "Robert, Sharron, Stephen, and Michael are flying in tonight. David and Amie are coming soon. Hold on."

Walking out of Bloomington Hospital into the early morning hours, delighting in the sun rising, I spin around, repeating the words of a Lakota Chief: "Today is a good day to die."

Julie visits Poppa, hoping he can hear her words of appreciation for the life he has shared with her, Richard, and others. Now and again, he looks at her and attempts a few words she can't make out.

"You're a good man, Sol Balaban. You've made a difference in the world. You've helped a lot of people with your kindness and generosity. And you're one funny guy.

"Robert, Sharron, Michael, and Stephen will be here tonight. They want to say good-bye. They'll be here soon. Hang on,' she says.

Poppa squeezes her hand—a solid squeeze. Julie knows he heard her.

Even as Poppa labors breath by breath, this impatient man waits until enveloped by his loving circle.

At 8:30 that night, Robert, Sharron, Stephen, and Michael arrive. Amie and David are there. Each kisses him and tells him he's loved. All laugh and cry over him.

Robert later tells me that the grandchildren all seem mildly uncomfortable, but also accept that they are witnessing the end of a life. Somehow understanding that they too, are part of this cycle of living and dying.

Thirty minutes later, with deep peace, quiet, and no pain, he dies.

Julie and Mom were in the hallway.

I arrive shortly afterwards.

I walk into the room with David.

The air is thick and still.

Poppa is gone, but I sense his soul hovering above him after the last rattled breath left his lungs.

Where does the soul go? I have read that it has actual weight, though infinitesimal.

While I have no sense of that space called heaven, an image of my father and mother eventually reuniting brings me a sense of peace, no matter its truth.

I hold the hand of my father, Poppa Sol.

I hold the warm hand of my son, David.

I look outside.

Stars are shining through a thin cloud cover.

The moon is cut in half.

The street is empty except for a lone car driving by.

ACKOWLEDGMENTS

The Quarry Writers inspired openness, productivity, and creativity over many years: Mark Albrecht, Vic Gregor, Dianne Haaga, Mary Anne Herrick, Clement Soffer, Marylyn Tymon, June Utecht, and Judy Warren.

The Bloomington Writers provided valuable comments. They include Julie Bloom, Carolyn Geduld, Audrey Heller, Jackie Oleneck, and Leon Olereck.

I want to thank Gina Anderson, Steve Arnold, David Balaban, Robert Balaban, Stephen Balaban, Matt Bloom, Bea Camiener, Michelle Decker, Susie Deutch, Doug Eck, Ray Hedin, Douglas Hofstadter, Mike Horvath, Jeff Isaac, Keith Kelly, Lois Klein, Mark Lee, Norman Levine, Julia Livingston, Ronald Lustig, Joan McIntosh, Amie Neff, Steve Parrington, Eric Rensberger, Phil Stafford, Darrell Stone, Robert Venners, Jr., and Joan White for their contributions to this book.

Jody Curley helped me capture Poppa Sol's adult day care experience.

Holly Stocking helped clarify for me the interplay of facts, truth-telling, and the unknown in creative non-fiction.

Much gratitude goes to Marcia Cebulska for her friendship and for enhancing my writing in too many ways to enumerate. My Flint Hills Publishing editor extraordinaire, Paul Fredrickson, helped me shape this story with his empathy and expertise. Thea Rademacher put it all together!

Special thanks to Julie Bloom for her love and support throughout the decades of birthing this book.

ABOUT THE AUTHOR

Richard Balaban, PhD, is a son, husband, father, grandfather, and clinical psychologist. He taught special education, was the Coordinator of the Children and Youth Service at a community mental health center, and has a decades-long private practice.

He has taught in the Psychology Departments at S.U.N.Y. at Buffalo and Indiana University (IU), and in the School of Public and Environmental Affairs at IU. He has presented at national conferences such as American Psychological Association and American Group Psychotherapy Association. With Chris Chouteau and Julie Bowden, he co-authored *The Last Workshop*, a novel about the numerous workshops he co-led at Esalen Institute, in Big Sur, California.

www.flinthillspublishing.com/richard-balaban